GIVE

16 Giving Strategies to Grow Your Business

By Sam Rathling

http://samrathling.com

Endorsements for "GIVE" from Best-Selling Authors

"The ultimate guide for using giving as a basis to build stronger, deeper business relationships, increased referrals, and a more successful business, this book takes the Givers Gain® philosophy of helping others to an entirely new level. Offering fresh, results-oriented perspectives and strategies for business growth, Sam Rathling outlines highly practical, actionable steps which every business owner will benefit from and can easily implement within the framework of their business. This is without a doubt one of the must read business books of the year." **Ivan Misner, Ph.D., NY Times Bestselling Author and Founder of BNI®**

"I always tell my clients to forget about the selling & think about how you can help others. The mindset for success is to come from a position of helping. Helping is an attitude that wins and is sustainable over the long term. It's not the latest "marketing craze" that everyone will get wise to...people need help, want help & appreciate help. What Sam Rathling has done in this book is detail exactly how to go about helping and hence winning. Before you start saying you are too busy already to do more...wait, Sam also has answers for that on getting more efficient & making more time." **Mark Rhodes, Mentor, Speaker and Author of "Think Your Way to Success" & "How to Talk to Absolutely Anyone"**

"This book points out that to grow your business you have to give to others. The more you do that, the more they give to you. Because most people don't give in this way (let's face it, people rarely give to us unless we ask them to, demand they do or we pay them), acting this way ensures you stand out. This book helps you become an expert giver (and, by default, benefit from others' reciprocations). In

effect, Sam Rathling is endorsing her favourite Walt Disney quote: 'Observe the masses. Do the opposite'. Her message is clear and persuasive: the more we give, the more people reciprocate, helping you both grow your businesses. It's just the way it is." **Andy Bounds, Best-Selling Author of "The Jelly Effect" and "The Snowball Effect"**

"As someone whose success in business and in life has come from a core value of giving to others, (called a Givingpreneur in the book), I was delighted to discover GIVE to be a different type of book. Unlike the thousands of books that offer complicated and complex "systems" or those which are overly "feel good" in nature, Sam Rathling provides a simple, easy-to-read book full of 16 brilliant, practical pieces of advice. Being truly authentic to her giving message, the book comes chock-full of free online resources and templates for your use. Although it is geared towards a business audience, the lessons are very helpful for everyone as they transcend business life and into daily life. So if you're looking for a delightful read with a strong message that's easy to implement, give GIVE a go!" **Tim Houston, Best-Selling Author of "The World's Worst Networker: Lessons Learned by the best, from the absolute worst!"**

Table of Contents

Dedication

This book would not have happened without the special people in my life. To my Mum & Dad for everything they do, have done to support and encourage me.

To my amazing husband for keeping me grounded and loving me unconditionally. Finally to my incredible children Oscar, Maya and Liliana for keeping me young at heart and bringing positivity, fun, laughter and light into my world.

Who Was This Book Written For?

To the business owners and entrepreneurs out there looking for new ways to grow your business, I wrote this for you. Ever wondered why your business plan or company goals are not being met? Do you really understand why all of your focus on *getting* sales, *getting* into profit and *getting* new clients is not yielding the results that you really want or really deserve?

This book is about to re-shape your thinking when it comes to goal-setting, relationship building, networking and your sales pipeline. This book was written for you if you want new ideas and a solid foundation for action and results.

I have been there, and have faced the struggles that every business owner goes through. I have experienced the highs and the lows, and the emotional rollercoaster that comes with running your own business. Now I am ready to share with you the key to unlocking more business opportunities than you can imagine without spending any money on advertising, marketing or staff, simply by shifting your mind set and your approach to the way you do business.

I am going to give you some amazing ideas that you won't find in the traditional 'How To' sales and marketing books, nor will you find these ideas being taught in business schools. Why? Because the business world is all about 'getting'. We are constantly bombarded with information about how to get more clients, more followers, more visibility, more sales, more profits, when all it takes is a move to the Giving Mindset.

If you really want to achieve success then this book is for you. If you are fed up with the same old information about how to grow your business, then I am excited that you decided to pick up or download this book. The topics and action plans I cover in this book will help you to become one of the many 'Givingpreneurs' across the globe who are achieving amazing results by focusing on giving as a way of doing business.

What if you could give as a strategy to gain everything that you want in your business and life? This book is about giving you practical business strategies that involve giving in order to create the wealth and success that you deserve. The 16 ideas you are going to explore in this book will open your mind to a giving mind-set that will lead you to greater profits, more success and increased happiness.

Chapter 1 - The Giving Mindset

"It's not that successful people are givers; it is that givers are successful people." **Patti Thor**

One of the first ever lessons I learnt when I started out in business involved giving. I was on the receiving end, and it happened shortly after my first ever business networking event, shortly after I set up my first company in 2005. At a business breakfast event, I met with a Printer named Patrick Hughes. He seemed very friendly and well-connected and we exchanged business cards on that morning.

Within 24 hours of meeting Patrick, he had been in touch with me by email and phone, and had arranged to meet me for a coffee. He had found out that I was not only starting up a new recruitment business but that I was also in a brand new country. I had moved to Ireland in 2005, and I only knew one person there, my husband, and my husband didn't know anyone locally either so I faced a big challenge ahead.

I met Patrick a couple of days later, and he spent an hour and a half learning all about my business, finding out more about me as a person, and asking how he could help me. This included the type of clients I was looking for specifically. I actually thought there had to be some kind of catch, especially when I turned to him after an hour and said, so how can I help you? His reply was, "We'll get to me some other time, the purpose of this meeting was for me to help you, don't worry about me."

At the time, it was very alien to me, here was a person I had just met, in a brand new place, and he was being so helpful and wanting to help me? It felt very strange and I was a bit sceptical. However, what Patrick did that week was to give me my first education on how to network effectively, he followed up (one of only 16 people I met that day who did) and he understood that to get more business, and that is to focus on giving and helping others.

Before long Patrick was my Printer and I was passing him business, and after three months he gave me a referral to my first multi-national client. I later learnt that Patrick was a member of BNI, and he was the reason I ended up walking through the door of a BNI chapter, where I learnt all about the power of Givers Gain®. You'll be learning more on that in a moment.

Why Do I Live to Give?

From a young age I have had a giving mind-set. I was very lucky to have been surrounded by a loving and giving family, and one of the most influential people in my life was my grandmother, Alma Rose. Alma was one of the most inspiring and giving people I have ever known. The best giving story I ever heard about my Nan involved my Grandad and his love for a bet at 'the dogs' or greyhound racing, a popular betting sport in the UK. Grandad decided in his infinite wisdom that it would be a good idea to bet all of his holiday savings on a dog that his mate Alfie said was a 'dead cert', or in non-cockney slang, definitely going to win!. Bear in mind that the holiday was due to happen the following week with 2 very excited children, my Dad and my Uncle. This was either really smart or really stupid!

Grandad and Alfie held their breath as the race started, silence descended on the stadium as the six dogs leapt out of their traps. Dog number six, the 'dead cert' led from the start, and as he turned the last corner, number four crept up beside him and the crowd roared their dog home, Grandad and Alfie willing number six to hold on to his lead. As the dogs crossed the line, it was too close to call. The dogs had finished the race side by side in a photo finish. They waited and waited for the stewards to assess and announce the winner. Then the announcement came over the tannoy, "The winner of Race 9 is Dog Number Four!!!"Grandad and Alfie looked at each other and the reality of what just happened, hit home. Grandad had lost all of the holiday savings by a nose.

Grandad had to head home with no savings left and the knowledge that he now had to explain what had happened to my Nan. You can imagine what most unforgiving spouses would say in this situation, most words I could not repeat on paper here! What my Nan did, truly encapsulates her attitude to life and giving. Instead of shouting, getting angry and generally making Grandad feel even worse than he already did, she simply said "George, don't worry, I'll give you all of the money I have, and tomorrow we'll go back to the dogs and win the holiday money back." So they did and the next night at Catford Dogs in South East London, they won 6 out of the 9 races and won all the savings money back and more, using the money that my Nan had been saving as a surprise for my Grandad.

Although my Nan was never a business woman, I am certain that she would have applied all of her relationship building, people skills and giving attitude to any situation and would have been a great success. Her love of helping others has really rubbed off on me, and even before I knew about giving as a business strategy I have been applying it for most of my adult life.

I absolutely love giving, it is part of my DNA and inherent in my personality. Such amazing events and circumstances have come about for me both personally and professionally because of my ability to give. I can directly associate sales into the millions in my separate businesses in the last 7 years. I am going to share how I was able to do that directly through giving activity in this book.

Many people associate giving purely with charitable donations and philanthropy, but there is so much more to explore in business when it comes to giving. Everything I have learnt about giving as a business strategy is within this book and I hope that you too will see an increase in sales from the strategies you will learn here.

Givers Gain®

I have been in business as a self-employed entrepreneur since 2005 and before that spent some time in the corporate world working for drinks giant Diageo, and across both experiences I have seen that there are only really two main types of people, givers and takers. Another description would be farmers and hunters.

Takers are driven, hungry, ambitious people who let nothing stand in their way of their success and goals. Every business relationship they establish is about what's in it for them. This selfish approach is usually well suited to a sales environment, and is often driven by a combination of money, commissions and the next rung on the corporate ladder.

An easy way to spot a taker is at a networking event, they hunt the room looking to give away as many business cards or fliers as possible. Their sole purpose for being there is to see if they can pick up a new client and it's all about GET, GET, GET. There is limited focus on relationship-building and these people typically have a high number of connections in their network but a shallow depth of relationship with any of them.

Givers can be just as driven as takers, but the way that they approach business relationships, is to focus on the people around them. It's about what they can do for others, in the knowledge that their acts of giving will come back to them in more ways than one.

The mind-set of a giver is unselfish and this approach leads them to greater success.

Networks of givers can also be wide and diverse, but the difference is that they know how to leverage their networks and have deep rooted relationships with a small number of the people within their network and they are able to generate business by farming those relationships through acts of giving and helping others.

"Giver's Gain"®, is the philosophy of the world's largest and most successful referral organisation, BNI (Business Network International). Dr. Ivan Misner who founded BNI over 25 years ago says the following about this widely known business philosophy:

'Good networking involves providing a positive and supportive environment to other business people. Notable networking is predicated upon the concept that givers gain. If you freely give business to others, they will give business to you. This concept is based on the age-old notion that "what goes around, comes around. If I give business to you, you'll give business to me, and we will both do better as a result. Networking is like a savings account: if you keep investing wisely, you can draw upon it when you need it.'

Wikipedia refers to this term when applied to small business networking, as helping business owners to function at their best, as business owners working together to give to each other and bring in new customers. When people focus on others instead of themselves in business networks, it will create an image of one who helps other people. Others will in return want to help them. Thus the givers are also gaining from the experience.

Whether you chose this book because you already like helping others and are already in some ways applying giver's gain or whether you have up until now focused more on getting, I know that you will benefit from the strategies in this book and I cannot wait to share with you the information which is going to transform your way of thinking and your mindset to giving in your business.

Chapter 2 - Giving Goals

"We make a living by what we get, but we make a life by what we give." **Winston Churchill**

Every business owner knows that goal-setting is an important part of their business. Goals help us to focus, to get things done and to reach for targets that will help the business to grow. Think about your own business goals, they probably involve gaining new clients, getting more sales and achieving a certain amount of profit. You may also set goals around your team, new products and services as well as goals for your marketing efforts. All of these are great goals to have and I would encourage every business owner to regularly write down goals and review them. For the purpose of this chapter, we'll call these 'getting goals'.

This chapter however, is all about a different set of goals. This is about setting goals that actually focus on helping others. By focusing on activities that help other people, you will suddenly open yourself up to a chain of events and opportunities that come back to you through a new focus on giving. These are your 'giving goals'.

I have set my own giving goals for the last 5 years and I have been overwhelmed with the results. I have my own personal giving goals, and have since extended these out to my team. The staff who work alongside me are not tasked with getting either, they too have giving goals. This for me has been one of the most effective ways to bring in new business. When I give keynote presentations across the world this is one of the tips that I share and it always gets the most positive feedback from audiences. It is such a new way of thinking about your business.

In this chapter I am going to give examples of the type of giving goals that you could set for your business. Many of those listed below are explored in much greater detail in the other chapters of this book. For now this is a simple glance at some of the activities that could yield you significant results.

Some of the types of giving goals you could set include:

- The number of referrals you want to give to other people in your network

- The number of 'acts of giving' that you want to participate in eg. Giving advice or support to others who need it

- The number of handwritten thank-you cards you want to send out each week or month

- The number of presentations or speaking slots you would be willing to give free of charge to help another person

- The number of clients you want to give a gift to this year

- The number of 'giving meetings' do you want to hold each month

- The number of voluntary hours or days you want to give to your community

- The number of blogs, articles or e-books you want to write to share information that would help others

- The number of useful articles will you share with other people through your social media outlets

- The number of testimonials or recommendations will you give to others

- The number of people you want to help through mentoring

Your initial reaction to this list is probably "Where on earth am I going to get the time to do any of this!!???". On first glance all of these activities look like they would take up your time and take you away from those getting goals which you are used to focusing on. The reality is that these activities will actually massively impact on your ability to grow your business, and you will find that you no longer need to look for new business, you will attract it to you through a powerful network of connections that want to reciprocate back to you.

If you feel like you have a time famine at the moment, then in 'Chapter 5 – Giving Time' I will be sharing some top tips to help you get some time back in your business and in 'Chapter 11 – Giving Responsibility' we will be looking at how you can delegate and outsource to help you grow your business.

Right now though, I am going to share with you some of the giving goals that myself and my team use to drive our business, the giving goals that we set are for the entire team, from Company Directors through to sales people and administration staff.

Example Giving Goals (Per Annum)

Referrals To Other People:	350 (Average 1 per week)
Thank You Cards Sent Out:	260 (Average 5 per week)
Number of Giving Meetings:	150 (Average 3 per week)
Recommendations given:	50 (Average 1 per week)
Free speaking events:	5 (Average 1 every 2 months)
Free Mentoring of others:	5 (5 people chosen annualy)
Giving Connections to Others:	50 (Average 1 per week)
Acts of Giving:	100 (Average 2 per week)
Number of Business Blogs:	50 (Average 1 per week)

Number of Articles Shared:	365 (Average 1 per day)
Number of Volunteer Hours:	100 (Average 2 hours weekly)
Number of Charities to Support:	2 (We pick two every year)

So these are typically some of the goals we set as a team. Not only do we write these down but we also track them every week to ensure that we are going to achieve them. Later in this book you will be given a link to download a template for an 'Activity Success Tracker' which features all of these giving goals and more, to help you focus on the types of activities that will yield results. You can find this in Chapter 5 - Giving Time, I purposefully did not include a link to that document here as there are a number of items on the Activity Success Tracker that need to be explained before you take a look at it. In addition, the chapter on giving time will also show you how to free up your time in order to make space for more giving activities.

The idea around giving goals may require a complete shift in your company culture, especially if you work in a commission based or sales driven environment. Having spent 11 years in the recruitment industry, before I turned to writing and speaking, I was in one of the most commission driven environments I have ever experienced. Although on the surface, recruitment may seem a giving activity because you are helping others to secure jobs, the reality is that it is very different. The targets I was given as a recruiter before I ran my own agency were all about sales, getting, hunting and doing everything possible to close a deal.

It was not to my liking at all, which is why when I set up my own recruitment business I decided never to pay a single piece of commission to any of my team. With the commission and getting element stripped out, the experience for the clients and the candidates was much more focused on farming relationships and delivering great service, rather than get, get, get all the time. It was much easier to introduce the concept of giving goals in this environment and my team loved the fact that they were not on strict targets and constantly feeling under pressure to close a deal.

Now all of my businesses and teams are based on farming relationships, account management and a total focus on the customer and other people in our networks. Giving is part of our culture, so referrals, saying thank-you and connecting others is natural to every team member.

Actions & Ideas on Giving Goals

1. Take a look through the list of giving goals and decide which giving activities you could commit to

2. Ask your team (if you have staff) to think about the different ways that they could give

3. Go back over your getting goals, refine them and add in your giving goals

4. Write the goals down and make a commitment now to achieving them.

Chapter 3 - Giving Meetings

"I have found that among its other benefits, giving liberates the soul of the giver." **Maya Angelou**

In the previous chapter on giving goals, we looked at setting goals for activities that primarily revolve around helping another person. In this chapter we will explore the concept of a giving meeting. In the beginning of this book I shared with you my story upon first arriving in Ireland. Do you remember Patrick, who I met first at a networking event, then arranged to meet me for a coffee? Patrick and I are still in touch and he is a very valued client in my business, he now works in international sales for ASEA, (an amazing product), and is no longer in the print industry. Do you recall that he spent 90 minutes in that meeting focusing 100% on me and what he could do to help me? That is what I now refer to as a giving meeting and this is how I approach every new connection and prospective referral partner or potential client.

This again may involve a shift in your mindset and way of thinking about the meetings that you hold from now on. Because every sales training presentation you attend and many books you read about how to get new business involve how you can get your sales message across to the other person. Often you will read or hear tips on how to communicate your features and benefits to them in a way that helps them to buy from you. Yes there is some focus on the other person, but this usually involves asking questions to understand their needs so that you can hen pitch your solutions, products or service to the person in front of you.

The giving meeting is an act of helping another person. The sole purpose of your time you spend with the other person is to understand their business, and what you can do to help them first. A real giving meeting is a 100% dedication to the other person and their business.

This chapter will give you a template to work from with a set of questions that will enable you to really give and help them. In order to help the other person you need to understand their business and open up opportunities for you to help them, refer them and create a long-lasting relationship.

The Giving Meeting Template

The following questions are to be used in a giving meeting to establish rapport, build the relationship and understand how you can help them. Once you know this information about the other person and you feel comfortable referring them to your network then it will be much easier for you to help them in some way:

Question 1 - Tell me about yourself and how you got into this business

This question allows you to relax the other person, they will feel comfortable sharing their background and history and you can learn a lot from the person by having them talk about what they did before. The advantage for you is that you get to find out what contacts the person may have based on their previous career. You are not going to use this information now, but it should be stored and recorded after the meeting. When you have helped this person first, they will want to help you back in the future. By understanding their contacts from past roles, you may secure an opportunity of an introduction further down the line.

Question 2 - What is it that you love about what you do?

This question allows the person you are trying to help to talk about their passion. You will quite often see body language change and a more animated response. Everyone loves to talk about their passions and what they love to do. This again is part of the relationship building process. If you know what they love about their work, you know that they will be most responsive when you refer them a contact or a piece of business which involves what they love to work on.

Question 3 - What are the main products and services you offer to clients?

This question is more of a fact-finding exercise. If you've not had a chance to do your homework on the company before the meeting then this is an opportunity to learn about the products and services on offer.

Question 4 - After you have delivered your products /services what results does the client see?

This is really asking the question what value do you add. This should be where you find out the benefits of working with the company you are trying to help. Quite often the products and services are the main focus of a meeting like this, but if you truly want to help the person then you need to know how they deliver results for their clients. Do they save client's money? Do they reduce stress? Do they give peace of mind? It is really finding out what the clients they work for are left with after they have delivered their service or products. What do they feel, think, do or have AFTER the company has delivered their work.

Question 5 - What makes you totally unique and different from your competition?

This is all about USP's (Unique Selling Points). The person you are meeting needs to clearly communicate their points of difference if you are going to be able to help them. The issue is that most small businesses cannot really identify their absolute unique selling points. They use descriptions like 'we give really personal service', however that really is not a unique selling point. It may be true, but all of their competition is out there saying that too.

Question 6 - What professions or categories of business are you looking to talk to?

This question is all about identifying potential strategic alliances or referral partners for the person you are trying to help. You could introduce them to an end customer who spends with them once, or you could introduce them to a connection who could pass them multiple clients. An example of this would be a video production company. You could introduce them to an SME who wants to make a video for their website, or even better would be to introduce them to a marketing agency who outsource all of their video production work. Which is the more valuable contact? The second one of course because of the potential number of clients that it could bring. The more you help them with strategic alliances and referral partners, the more will come back to you.

Question 7 - What are the names of the top 20 companies you would love to do business with?

This is a question that many small business owners cannot answer off the top of their head. Quite often the target market for a company starts with 'Anyone who...' or 'Any company that...'. If you can get a list of the dream clients that the person in front of you is looking to do business with than you can be much more specific in your quest to help them. Go back to the giving meeting I had with Patrick, he asked me this question but I was prepared and had already created a top 100 prospect client list from business directories and LinkedIn. I was able to name companies that I wanted to work with and he was able to facilitate an introduction for me to someone on the list. If the person you are meeting is not prepared, ask them to list for you the last 10 customers they did business with. This will give you a chance to see the types of companies that they help. In addition the assumption would be that if they have already done business with one haulage/logistics company that they would like to be introduced to more haulage and logistics companies. Then you can start to help them be more specific.

Question 8 - What questions can I ask a potential client to help open up the opportunity for you?

You could be standing in the middle of a referral opportunity for the person in front of you, but unless you know what to say in the situation you could blow it. This question is really to get an idea of what the person you are trying to help would say if they met someone looking to buy their product or service. By having 2 or 3 key questions to qualify the opportunity you will make it much easier to pass on the person's details to a potential client. It also means that the referral is more likely to happen and be the kind of opportunity that they are looking for because you have been armed with the right questions to ask.

I have an electrician in my network who I use personally and refer to other people. He helps companies to reduce their electricity bill through an energy audit. Every time I see spotlights in a venue, office, or house I simply ask "Do you know how much those are costing you?". This starts a conversation and allows me to move into a potential referral situation where I can help him with a new client.

Question 9 - How can I introduce you? What do you want me to say on your behalf?

If you can get a one liner, easy to remember from the person you are helping it will be so much easier to create an opportunity for them. For the electrician I simply say "I know a great electrician who can save you up to 80% on your electricity bill through a free energy audit. I highly recommend him and he's saved me a fortune!". When you are in your giving meeting, try to identify what to say on behalf of the person you are helping to make it easy to refer them.

This is especially important if they work in the type of business where everyone already has a supplier such as an Accountant or a Printer. It has to be more compelling than just "I know a great [insert profession] can I get him to give you a call?"

Question 10 - Can you tell me a story about how you recently helped a client?

If you are stuck on question 9, or if the person you are meeting is stuck then this may help. Facts tell and stories sell, so this is where you can get the person to share success stories and how they help their clients.

From this you may also find a good one liner introduction. It is far easier to remember a compelling story than a list of features and benefits, and combine this with emotion and you will have an easy way to help the person, simply by relaying the great story about how they help their clients.

Question 11 - What am I going to hear or see in my everyday settings that could indicate an opportunity for you?

This last question is really to help you determine triggers that you may see or hear when you are out and about that will make you think of this persons business. If you go back to the electrician, he has trained me to look out for spotlights whenever I am in people's homes or in commercial premises such as a hotel or an office. He knows how much he can save a venue or household. So every time I see spotlights I think of the electrician. Armed with my one question "Do you know how much those are costing you?", combined with my how to introduce you "I know a great electrician who can save you up to 80% on your electricity bill through a free energy audit. I highly recommend him and he's saved me a fortune!"

Question 12 - Where do you network?

This is a great question to ask a new person in your network, they may be attending events that you were not aware of and they may be happy to take you along and introduce you to potential new contacts. Share each others interests and networks outside of the main business and you never know what you might uncover. Either way it will really help you to form a strong relationship, find common ground and lead to future opportunities.

So you get to the end of the giving meeting, and now you have lots of information gathered from the other person. The final thing to do is to close the meeting by summarising back to the person what information you have taken down. You could also then arrange a follow up meeting date where you agree to meet up for a second time to go through the actions arising from this first meeting. It is likely that during the 12 questions you determined a number of ways to help the other person. Now it's all about follow up. The most important thing is that if you agreed to take action or do something for them that you actually do it. Having this follow up meeting brings some accountability in and will ensure that you DWYSYAGTD! (Do What You Say You Are Going To Do!).

The Giving Meeting Template Download

To make things easy for you and to help you with your Giving Meetings, I have created a template for you to download. Simply visit this link and you can download a free PDF template for you to use in your giving meetings.

http://samrathling.com/giving-meeting-template

One suggestion I have for you to make your giving activity produce results, is that you create a document for your own business using this template of questions too. Imagine at the end of a giving meeting the person you are helping asks how they can help you back, or later in the relationship they are looking to help you in some way. The best thing to do is be prepared for this as it will happen.

The 121 Toolkit Template Download

My recommendation is to send back your version of these questions in a document so that they have a complete overview of your business and how they can help you. Imagine if every time you met someone new in your network, that they took away with them the list of answers to these 12 questions for your business.

Once again, I am going to make this real easy for you (a theme running throughout this book!). You can download an editable word document for you to complete for your own business, I call this a 121 Toolkit. It's something you can use in both giving meetings and in other meetings that involve you presenting your business to a potential referral partner, strategic alliance, supplier or client.

I have been using this myself for years, and more recently have been giving this to clients and other people in my network and to date it has produced some staggering results. One of the best stories I know about this document involves a lady based in Manchester in the UK. She had been struggling to get new clients into her alternative healing business. People in her network just didn't 'get' her business and didn't know how to refer her.

After hearing about this 121 Toolkit, she created this document for her business in preparation for a 10 minute presentation she was giving the following week to her networking group. At the end of the presentation she gave a copy of this 121 Toolkit to the group to take away with them. Bear in mind, she had not received a single referral in 7 months from this group of people. The week after giving the 121 Toolkit in hard copy to her networking group which detailed more specifically what she was looking for, she was given 19 referrals!! Yes, she went from zero referrals in 7 months, to 19 in just one week! Now if that story doesn't motivate you to get one of these for your business then you may as well stop reading now, because there is more great stuff to come in the other chapters too.

You can download your 121 Toolkit template here:

http://samrathling.com/121-toolkit-template

So now you know how to make your giving meetings work for you, and of course the person you are looking to help with their business. In addition you have a great tool to use for your own business to really focus the people in your network on how they can help you back. It can take some time to put together a great 121 Toolkit but it is well worth the effort for the results it will deliver back to your business.

Next we are going to spend some time on Giving Gratitude, as I am sure when you start giving help to others you will start to hear the words 'Thank You' a lot more, and you will also need some great ideas on how to say 'Thank You' to others when the new opportunities and clients start rolling in to your business.

Actions & Ideas on Giving Meetings

1. Think about 3 people you have recently met that you could hold a giving meeting with and write down their name.

2. Visit the link and download the giving meeting template, start using this with all new connections you meet.

3. Create your own version of a 121 Toolkit so that you have something to give a person when they ask how they can help you back.

Chapter 4 - Giving Gratitude

"Remember, that the happiest people are not those getting more, but those giving more." **H. Jackson Brown Jr.**

Saying "Thank You" is one of the most powerful and effective ways to generate business. I still remember receiving a hand-written thank you card from someone who I had given a referral to. It had a positive quote on the inside and a customised picture specific to their business on the front. I was so touched that someone had taken the time to send this to me, it felt amazing to receive that card. Ever since then I have integrated gratitude into my business. It is one of the significant ways to help you to stand out from your competition as unfortunately such a small number of businesses do this well.

Today, one of our company goals is to send at least ten 'thank you' cards per week. Recognising people's efforts motivates them to want to help you more. In addition, the word-of-mouth about you and your company will spread. They will talk about you more, the card may even sit proudly in their office and you will be remembered. Thanking your network is a critical aspect of being an excellent networker. It sounds really obvious and simple, but it is very rare to find in business.

Let's first look at some everyday opportunities to say "Thank You":

- A brand new customer decided to use your product/service

- An existing customer gave you repeat business

- A member of your team went above and beyond the call of duty

- A supplier exceeded your expectations

- Someone gave you an excellent referral

- You were given an amazing opportunity which has led to more business

- A journalist published an article about your business

- You were sent a gift by someone

- You were given some really good advice by a mentor or business advisor

- You were given some exposure online by a good contact

- Someone wrote a great testimonial about your business

- You were connected to a new contact and now have a great opportunity

- You were invited to an event which was beneficial to you

- Someone gave you a book to read which transformed your business

- You heard a fantastic speaker who had a major impact on you

Have a look through this list, and if there is an occasion in this list which you can relate to why not decide to take action and send some thank-you cards out. You do not need to look far for an opportunity to say thanks. I always have a stack of "Thank You" cards which have a picture on the front, taken by an amazing documentary photographer, Roger Overall, who refers me a lot of business. On the inside is a positive quote, reference to Roger's picture and website, and on the back I feature my logo and contact details.

Every time I send out a card, I am also giving visibility to Roger, helping him to gain more exposure with every card I send. For less than $100 I can print 500 customised cards to make a huge difference to my bottom line. You can start with cards, but the thank you does not have to be a simple card. Let's look at some obvious ways to say "Thank You":

- Send Flowers

- Send Chocolates

- Send a gift voucher

- Send them a book with a hand-written message inside

- Send wine or champagne

- Send a hand-written letter

- Give them a testimonial about their business

- Offer your product or service free of charge

- Take the person out for lunch or dinner

Think back to the last time someone gave you any of the above gifts, and I don't mean for a birthday or anniversary present! I mean in business. How did it make you feel? What impact could this have on your customers? What impact could this have on the contacts in your network if you increased your level of activity in saying thank you?

Now think back to the last time that you gave any of the items on this list to others. If you are struggling to think of a time, then it has definitely been too long!   The ripple effect that this creates in your network is incredible.

Now let's look at some more creative ways to say "Thank You":

- Send a very powerful video email

- Gift an App (for those contacts who have an iPad or an iPhone)

- Arrange to get the persons Car valeted

- Arrange for a Spa Treatment or gift a Spa Voucher

- Create a customised certificate, frame it and send it

- Subscribe them to a magazine for their business

- Send free tickets to an event

- Send an audiobook

- Put on a free seminar and invite your clients

- There are many creative ways to show you care, the list goes on.

Recognition of people's efforts, and showing gratitude for what they do for us, has really helped our business to grow. More people remember and refer us because we always say thank-you.

To help you with this I am going to give you a few specific examples of how gratitude is integrated into our company culture.

Example 1 – Saying thank you to Customers

In the recruitment industry we have two types of customers. The most obvious is our clients, or the companies for whom we recruit for. The second is our candidates, who are just as important as our clients. Every time we place a candidate into a new job, within one week of their start date, we deliver a branded and personalised bottle of wine, all gift-wrapped to congratulate the candidate on their achievement and to thank them for working with us. Imagine the scene, it is your first week at work, you don't know anyone yet and it is a daunting experience. Then out of the blue, in walks your recruiter who has helped you secure the position and delivers a gift to your desk. The entire office stops, to see what is happening, and the impact of this one act of giving spreads throughout the business. Before long the new person is centre of attention in the office, and more importantly so is our brand.

A senior manager in a large multinational client, Victoria, still refers back to this act of giving. We regularly placed sales people and customer service staff with her call centre, she became a client in 2006, and every single time there was a new hire, we would walk in with our gift. Victoria has since changed companies but remains a client five years later having introduced us to her new employer. She refers to this personal touch in the testimonial which she provided.

"Samantha runs by far the best recruitment company I have ever worked with and consistently delivers outstanding results. Personable, friendly, professional and dedicated, she is committed to providing an excellent service and her company was always my number one choice for recruitment. Samantha added such a personal touch to her services, really caring about people and making sure that each and every hire was the right 'fit' for the job.

An absolute pleasure to work with, I couldn't recommend her highly enough."

This recommendation has since helped us to secure more clients, and a very loyal and happy customer. Candidates love this simple thank-you and it is also great for my recruitment team to help build relationships and maintain contact with both the client and our candidate base.

Example 2 – Saying Thank You to Journalists

I recently hired a PR company to help me gain visibility in the local and national newspapers for some significant milestones in the business. I was fortunate enough to have a half-page story with picture, run in the business section of the most widely read Irish Sunday newspaper. I was blown away with the coverage, so I decided to send a video email to the journalist who had never met me, as we conducted the interview over the phone. Here is the response back:

"Thank you so much for the message - most people don't even bother to email back to say they've seen the interview, and yours is definitely the first video message I've ever received. I'm glad you were happy with the piece, and hope it proves useful. Keep in touch and if you've any more interesting company news - new hires, new markets, investments etc. - make sure to let me know."
Dermot

Since that first article, I have been able to build a relationship with this journalist and have been given an opportunity to gain more visibility and increased coverage for my business, all because I said thank you when no-one else did.

Video email is a great way to say thank you, it is expressive, genuine and you can be alerted once the person has viewed your video email. My recommendation for this is Talk Fusion, there is a small cost involved, however the return on investment, if you use this new technology regularly, it is well worth it.

There are various video email software tools available so feel free to search online for other products, the point being that video email really is a fantastic way to say thanks. I use it for much more than saying thanks, and can be used for many other reasons such as follow up after networking events, rekindling relationships with customers and staying in touch with people who you don't see regularly.

Example 3 – Saying Thank You to Staff Members

My fantastic team are the most brilliant group of people to work with; they are so loyal, committed and driven to perform in the business. Without them we would not be able to achieve the results we have and I would not be in a position to pursue my passions and dreams. Every Friday in my business it is "Friday Club", that means taking the whole team out of the office for lunch to celebrate a great week and to help us get ready for the weekend. "Friday Club" is a weekly treat and this brings us all together to relax and build strong working relationships.

Last year, we had a challenging and demanding project for a client, which involved massive contribution from the team, and as a reward to say thanks we sent the project team off for an afternoon at the best local Spa, it was during the working week and they were absolutely blown away with the pampering and real treat that we had given them to say thanks for doing such an amazing job.

I am involved in a business mentoring group for some of the top female entrepreneurs in Ireland, and after hearing some of the ways in which I thank my staff, Regina decided to do the same. She organised for the team to come over to her house for what they thought was going to be an evening dinner party, and shortly after they had all arrived, a stretched limousine pulled up outside her house, whisked them all off for a night on the town and she treated them all to dinner, cocktails and of course a lift home in the limo!

The morale boost and increased productivity you can get from a simple (or extravagant) thank you is well worth the investment.

Having a "Thank You" Budget

This was an idea that I picked up from a great book *"The Thank You Economy"* by Gary Vaynerchuk. I now give my team a thank-you budget each year to empower them to give back to clients and referral partners to say thanks. They can use this budget any way they would like as long as the money is spent saying thank you. This both empowers the team and the customers love it too! This can really get creativity flowing in the team and enhances our giving gratitude, taking it to another level.

Giving gratitude is one of the most powerful and low cost strategies you can implement in your own business very quickly, and you will be amazed at the results. The simplest ideas are always the best! Enjoy saying thank you, it will change your mood and potentially your business too.

Actions & Ideas on Giving Gratitude

1. Order a stack of Thank You Cards and decide how many you plan to send out each week.

2. Think about 3 people who you've been meaning to thank recently and choose how you will say thanks.

3. If you have staff, when was the last time you said 'Thank You'? Decide how you will give them a treat.

4. Decide on your thank you budget and act on giving gratitude in the coming week.

Chapter 5 - Giving Time

"We must give more in order to get more. It is the generous giving of ourselves that produces the generous harvest."
Orison Swett Marden

Everyday life is getting faster and faster, there is a constant sense of rush and stress and much of this revolves around the fact that we simply don't have enough time to get everything done. This 'time-famine' puts us into reactive mode and leaves us little time to focus on the important things in life.

One of the best gifts you can give yourself is to give yourself the gift of time. Think about the last time that you gave yourself a day off. I'm talking about a day off where you relaxed and did something you enjoy doing, a day without the smartphone, emails and phone calls constantly distracting you.

I refer to these days in my world as 'Sammy Days'. This is a day for me, I can choose how I want to spend it, and usually this is my chance to unwind at a visit to the Spa, for a day of relaxation. I recommend having at least one 'Sammy Day' per month, the easiest way to plan this in is to note down what date in the month your birthday falls. My birthday is on the 4th of a month, so I choose to book off the 4th of every month as my day off. At least this way I know at the start of every year that I have planned in at least 12 days off for myself. By putting these into my diary and making sure that nothing gets in the way of these 12 days I am giving myself the gift of time.

I often come up with my most creative ideas on these days off, primarily because I am not caught up in the day to day rush and stress, and I am giving my brain time to think. Many people who have since adopted this concept of their day off being on the date of their birthday every month have also commented to me that this really does give them time to step back and focus. The key to making it work is putting the dates in your diary and not letting anything else get into your diary on that day.

How to Give Yourself More Time

Inbox Management seems to be one of the biggest causes of lost time for business owners and entrepreneurs everywhere. So I have a question for you: How many emails are currently in your inbox? Go on, be honest… 20, 40, 60, 100+. A never-ending inbox of emails is the cause for long working hours, stressed out entrepreneurs and procrastination. It is also the reason why so many people feel that they are so 'busy' all the time when in actual fact they are busy on the wrong things. A full and un-manageable inbox can distract you from what you know you really should be doing. This section features my top 10 tips for inbox management to help to keep your inbox to just 20 emails or less at any one time

Tip 1 – Still using Outlook? Stop! Get rid of it.

The quicker you move to a cloud based solution such as Google Apps for Business the better. My whole business changed for the better and we gained a wealth of time back for me and the whole team. For minimal cost, you can have your whole history of Outlook emails and all future emails on Google Apps. No more folders or searching for hours to find emails and seamless integration with many other Google features. It really is worth a look. You will save yourself and your team so much time by moving away from an Outlook mail platform.

Tip 2 – Take off any alerts visual or audio that tell you 'You've Got Mail!'

We simply can't resist the temptation to see who or what is in the email, so despite being in the middle of something really important we can't resist the temptation to jump across to the inbox. This simply creates a distraction and a loss of focus. I recommend that you turn off any pings or notifications that you've got a new email because your inbox is controlling you. The quicker you get control of your inbox back, the more productive you will become.

Tip 3 – Read emails in batches, set a diary appointment for 'Email Response'

Decide what two times of the day suits you best to read and respond to your emails. Now make an appointment in your diary and block out this time. It might be 9-10am and then 3-4pm. This may not be possible every day, but gain some consistency around when you check in to your mails. The rest of the day, don't even have your inbox open. If it's that urgent, they will call you! What email really can't wait just a few hours?

The problem is that you expect people to respond straight away and therefore you put yourself under massive pressure to respond straight away also. By getting some structure around your day you will find you are much more productive in between these two 'check-in' times.

Tip 4 – Four Choices – Delegate, Delete, Respond or File

To keep your inbox to a manageable less than 20, you should never read the same email more than once. Decide what to do with it there and then otherwise you will get bogged down.

Once you have read an email, your options are:

1. Delegate it – forward on for someone else to deal with

2. Delete it or archive it – to take it straight out of your inbox

3. Write back – most responses will only take 2 mins and these are the ones that can pile up

4. File it away – use folders in Outlook or labels in Google Apps to manage the emails

Treat your inbox as a to-do list, the only things left in there are the ones that you need to take action on. Then use coloured labels if you are using Google Apps, to help you visually see what the priority emails are. Everything else is gone from the inbox as quickly as possible. Your aim is to get it to under 20 at any one time.

Tip 5 – Use Rules and Organise Your Emails

If you regularly receive newsletters and updates from sources that you have subscribed to, then you have a number of ways to stop these from clogging up your inbox. You can unsubscribe to those that you never read. The ones you do want to read, but are not priority, you can set up rules in both Outlook and Google Apps, where the email actually skips your inbox and goes directly into a folder for you to review in your own time.

Tip 6 – Use the AwayFind App to still be alerted about urgent emails

If you are worried about only being on emails a couple of times a day, this App will help you to stay on top of urgent incoming mails. You can tell the App who your important people are and it can also sync with your calendar so it knows who you are meeting with in the coming days, so if an urgent email comes in, relating to an important client or a meeting you have coming up you no longer have to be in your inbox to know about it. You can get a text or other form of notification.

Download the AwayFind app at: http://www.awayfind.com/

Tip 7 – If you want to receive less emails, send less emails

It sounds obvious, but the reason many people receive lots of emails is because they spend so much time sending them out! If you reduce your output, it will have an impact on how many emails you receive. Try picking up the phone for a change, especially internally. If you have a team or colleagues, then how about getting up off your chair and walking over to their desk!! Email can often be the easy opt-out, try using other forms of communication and watch your inbox reduce.

Tip 8 – Use your 'Out of Office' Auto-Responder to manage expectations

When you are on holiday, you probably use an 'Out of Office' response to tell people you are away. When you come back you are faced with a mountain of emails and you feel very overwhelmed, and then because people know you are back, more and more emails keep coming! Next time you go away, put your out of office on 1 day earlier than your planned trip, and leave it on for 2 days longer that your anticipated return. This will give you time to breathe and catch up! Also why not continue to use the responder for your first week back. Mine normally says: "Thanks for your email. I have been out of the office for 2 weeks, so it may take me longer than normal to respond to emails come in during week commencing [Date]. I will get back to you as soon as I can, and if you have a very urgent enquiry please contact my office on [Number]. Thanks for your patience and understanding. You are simply managing expectations and you are not under pressure.

Tip 9 – Schedule Meetings in a more effective way

Use a free tool such as TimeTrade to schedule your meetings. Quite often your inbox can fill up with to-ing and fro-ing on simple diary arrangements. Timetrade.com links with your Google Calendar and many other calendar types including Outlook, using your real-time availability to help people schedule appointments with you. You set up an account and use their system to invite people to meet with you, on your time.

Click here to learn more about Timetrade: http://timetrade.com

Tip 10 – Use a Bridging Email where relevant

If you know that an email you have received is going to take longer than the time you have available today or even this week, send a short email to acknowledge that you have received the email. Advise the person when the earliest time you will be able to come back to them with an answer will be.

They will appreciate that you have taken the time to respond, and usually the timeframe you suggest will be acceptable. Now you have time to focus on your priorities, and you have not offended anyone, again you have space to breathe.

Giving Time to the Right Activities

Every business needs to know what activities drive sales. If you know what drives your sales you will always have a strong sales pipeline and know where to spend your marketing budget and more importantly, your time. If I were to ask you now, what percentage of your sales comes from the following activities would you know the % split for each?

- Attending Networking Events/Groups
- Word of Mouth Referrals
- Web or Phone Incoming Enquiries
- Strategic Alliances / Partners
- Pay per Click (PPC) Advertising
- Direct Marketing
- List Building & Inbound Marketing
- Cold Calling
- Adverts in the Paper or Online Ads (paid for and free)
- Existing Client Referrals
- LinkedIn personal and company profiles
- Facebook; Twitter; Google+; Pinterest & other Social Media
- Article Writing/Blogs
- PR / Press Releases
- Organic Search Traffic
- Other

So how did you get on? What % of your sales comes from each of the above activities? If you are not sure or only know the results for some of these, then it may help you to track and measure the impact of your sales and marketing efforts.

When you are able to get a handle on where your sales are coming from, you can then start to look at where to focus your efforts. Once you are clear on where the business is coming from, you can decide which activities you should give your time to in order to yield results. This is a very powerful way to grow your business.

To help you with this, I have devised an **Activity Success Tracker** for your business. My gift to you in this section is a free download of this business template so that you can start to track, measure and set targets for yourself based on your own business and activity. I won't even ask for your email address, just go straight into the download.

To download your free Activity Success Tracker you can visit:

http://samrathling.com/activity-success-tracker-download

Bear in mind that all of the tasks listed on the success tracker do not need to be completed by you on your own. If you have staff you can delegate many of these activities and if you are working on your own, why not consider outsourcing the work to freelancers. You can hire freelancers for a very low cost and give yourself the gift of time. You can learn more about this in 'Chapter 11 – Giving Responsibility'.

By measuring and tracking against targets you can easily see what tasks are working and where the sales are coming from. Allocate the referral source in your accounting system from now on, so that you are able to easily see where your sales efforts are most effective.

Giving Time to Family & Friends

Running a business can take up time, not only in the time that you are at work but headspace when you are not physically at work. The people who tend to suffer the most are our family and friends, especially when you are working long hours and even when you are home or around friends, you are clearly pre-occupied.

Making a conscious effort to leave work at the door when you come home will help this. Try the following ideas to give time to the most important people in your life:

- Switch off the smartphone and laptop when you walk in the door

- Go on 'Date Nights', take your spouse out by surprise, get a babysitter in and surprise them!

- Plan a day off, one of your 'Sammy Days' and choose to spend it with your family or friends

- If it is a long time since you had a holiday, book the time in your diary now for at least 2 weeks and spend an evening planning your dream holiday, show what you are working towards

- Create a vision board, this is a real family activity, sit down and cut out pictures from magazines of all of the things you want to see, do, own and experience – this could be material things such as cars, gadgets, houses etc. or they could be experiences such as trips of a lifetime, places you want to visit, things you all want to do. Hang the vision board in a place you can all see it, this way the family know why you are working as hard as you do. If you have kids, get them to create a vision board for themselves, and join in on your version.

- Make sure that you don't just stay in touch with friends via Facebook, plan a dinner party or night out on a regular basis to make time for your friends. Running a business can be consuming of your time and they need to know that you still care. They won't necessarily understand the pressures you are under if they are in a comfortable job as an employee.

Actions & Ideas on Giving Time

1. Plan in your equivalent of 'Sammy Day' dates into your diary, give yourself 12 days off in the coming year

2. Go through the list of 10 tips for effective inbox management and start applying these

3. Download the Activity Success Tracker and start to measure the effectiveness of your sales efforts

4. Give more time to the activities that are driving most of your sales

5. Go back over the last 12 months of sales and work out where they came from. Assign it to one of the 15 types of Sales and Marketing Activity listed in this chapter.

Chapter 6 - Giving Positivity

"I have found that among its other benefits, giving liberates the soul of the giver." **Maya Angelou**

As an Entrepreneur, it can be difficult sometimes to keep a positive frame of mind. If you are anything like I used to be, you find it hard to switch off, your brain is constantly thinking of new ideas even when you are not physically in work mode, your 'to-do' list is longer than your arm and you are constantly worrying about where the next sale is going to come from. Things don't always go your way in business and it can be tough to keep a positive mindset.

How To Keep A Positive Mindset

I remember having a conversation a number of years ago with my great friend and mentor, Iain Whyte from Big Man Talking after having a tough week in business and we were on our usual monthly coaching call. He made a suggestion which transformed my ability to stay positive in business for the long term.

He asked me how much time I spent in my car each week. At the time it was at least 12 hours a week in travelling to and from the office, going to meetings and sitting in traffic. He then asked me, what I listened to in the car during the course of those 12 hours per week. I said the local radio, news or music as I am sure most people would say. He then asked me whether the messages on the news and local radio were positive or negative?

Considering this conversation with Iain happened at the start of the recession the majority of the talk shows, news stories and information coming out the radio was highly negative. What came next transformed my business in so many ways that I will forever be grateful to Iain. He suggested that instead of listening to the local radio, news and music, that I start listening to audiobooks and podcasts related to business growth and success.

So my 12 hours a week of negativity, suddenly transformed into positive messages, I was learning every day, I was soaking up new ideas, new concepts, business models and success stories. What Iain gave me that day was the gift of positivity. I was already a positive person before this advice but what changed was the fact that I now had a way to translate my already positive outlook on life into my business.

My Smartphone now has at least 30 audio books loaded onto it at any one time, which I play in the car. I now avoid the news on the television, I don't read newspapers and I simply keep up to date with what's happening in the world through Twitter in small snippets (@samrathling).

Try it for a week and see what difference it makes to your level of positivity. Remove all media from your week to include the TV, newspapers, radio and just replace this time with podcasts and audio books. The iTunes University has some great material (mostly free) and you can listen to lectures on business from Stanford University and Harvard Business School. Audible.com has some great books and iTunes always has a great selection in the Business category.

Ever since that day I have continued to spread this idea to other business owners and Entrepreneurs in my network and amongst my clients. It is a message I regularly share in keynote presentations at conferences and events, thanks to Iain. I now get to give this gift of positivity to others and if it works for you then you can give the gift of positivity too.

People and Positivity

Have you ever thought how your interaction with others can affect their mood and their sense of positivity. Giving Positivity is one of the most gratifying ways to give to other people, compelling them to want to help you even more.

When you beam positivity and you always bring a ray of sunshine to the room, then you will be noticed more, and people will be more attracted to what you have to say. In the context of business, other Entrepreneurs will recognise you for being positive and giving a brighter perspective on things and this can only attract more people you and your business.

"How Full Is Your Bucket?" written by Tom Rath and Donald O. Clifton is a fantastic book which everyone in business owner and employee should read. How did you feel after your last interaction with another person? Did that person, your spouse, best friend, co-worker, or even a stranger "fill your bucket" by making you feel more positive? Or did that person "dip from your bucket," leaving you more negative than before? Organized around a simple metaphor of a dipper and a bucket, and grounded in 50 years of research, this book shows you how to greatly increase the positive moments in your work and your life — while reducing the negative.

One of my most favourite questions to use to fill other people's buckets is **"Has anyone told you how amazing you are today?"**. When I use this with people around me, they instantly smile and feel more positive, no matter what mood they started in before we spoke. Try it out and you'll love the results!

Giving a positive vibe and always injecting an infectious good mood into people can compel them to refer you more, do more business with you and want to be around you more. So have a think about your interactions this week, go and fill some buckets, make others feel amazing and watch your own positivity soar!

The people you surround yourself with can make a big difference to your mind set and level of positivity. One of the best ways to give to others is to bring a positive energy to a situation. There is nothing worse than being in a conversation with a 'fun-sucker'! You know the type, as soon as you meet them it's all doom and gloom, nothing is going right for them and they insist on drawing you into a conversation about how bad things are. My advice... if you have any of these types of people in your circles avoid them. You may come across these people at networking events, spot the signs early and run!

How to Attract More Positivity

Positivity is infectious! When positive things start to happen, then you often find that you attract more positivity and more success. If you consistently focus on the negativity, then guess what? More negativity will follow. I am a huge fan of "The Secret" by Rhondha Byrne. I have this audio amazing and inspiring book on my Smartphone all the time, the minute I can feel myself moving away from a positive mind set I listen to it to bring me back on track. The movie of the same book is equally as compelling if you prefer a more visual interpretation of it.

One of the ways that I breed positivity is to keep a Success Diary. This is a small, and in my case, bright and colourful book which I record my successes in, on a daily basis. What I write in my Success Diary can range from very small achievements to massive wins. The main thing is that at the end of every day I think about the most significant positive thing happened that day and write it down with the date against it. By focusing only on the positive areas of the day and recording them, it instantly attracts more success and positivity to the next day and so it goes on.

Why not try this out, keep a note of your positive outcomes from each day and see what happens. You can generate some great positive momentum by doing this one thing and making it a habit will breed positivity in your business. If you have staff, ask them to do the same, give them a Success Diary each and have them record their personal positive outcomes at the end of a day. They don't need to share this with anyone, it is a nice thing to do and they will appreciate you wanting them to be happier and more positive.

Positivity through Social Media

When it comes to social media and online networks, I always keep it positive. I only share articles and stories which are written in a positive light. By sharing positive news and focusing only on success when I am giving to my online networks, it affects others in a positive way too. I love sharing information and blogs about happiness, success and positivity. This is a great way to give to others and again gets people talking about your business. I find that my very positive tweets and updates always get shared as it makes others feel happy and positive too. If someone I am following on Twitter or a connection on LinkedIn regularly feeds negative news or comments I instantly unfollow them.

A great source of articles and blogs to share with your networks can be found in LinkedIn. The News Today section of LinkedIn has hundreds of blogs and articles from a whole range of industries and thought leaders. You can share updates across your LinkedIn,

Facebook, Google+ and Twitter networks and by keeping this all very positive you will attract more people to your business. I recommend sharing at least one article a day as a minimum and by using social media tools such as Hootsuite, you can share these positive messages across your networks in one place. Hootsuite can save you lots of time when it comes to managing your social media.

Find a few great blogs that always churn out positive news and articles that you know other people would love to read, then feed these to your social networks automatically to save you time. I recommend Twitterfeed, you can create an account and then link your Twitter, Facebook and LinkedIn accounts to regularly feed these articles out to your network automatically. You can set how frequently these feeds go out, and simply add the RSS feed from your chosen blog to start giving positivity without spending any time on it. It will look like you are on social media around the clock, it will keep you very visible to your online networks and you will not even have to think about it once this is set up.

Actions & Ideas on Giving Positivity:

1.Go on a Media Fast by cutting out Newspapers, TV & Radio.

2. Replace Media with audio books and Podcasts about Business and Success.

3. Set Up a Success Diary, write down the Positive Outcomes from each day.

4. Use the question "Has anyone told you how amazing you are today?" on at least 3 people.

Chapter 7 - Giving Back

"I don't think you ever stop giving. I really don't. I think it's an on-going process. And it's not just about being able to write a check. It's being able to touch somebody's life." **Oprah Winfrey**

This Chapter was written by Contributing Author: Beth Misner

I stood in front of the cooler filled with water bottles in the airport shop before boarding my flight. So many choices! Why do there have to be so many types of water to choose from? I mean, water is water, right? Wrong, apparently. There is water which is touted as being intelligent, water from glacial pools, water from volcanic pools, water from French springs, but in the short and sweet of it— I'm just thirsty! I want a drink of water.

I stood there for a few moments before one bottle caught my eye. In bright red letters the label read, "Education." The bottle beside it had a green label which read, "Health." Upon seeing these two bottles, my choice was made instantly. I reached in, took the one which said Education and made my way to the cash register.

I don't even know if it was priced higher than the intelligent, glacial, volcanic or spring waters. Do you know why? I didn't even look! I didn't care once I saw that this water bottling company gave back to education and health.

That started me thinking about conditioning and our current climate of a desire to give back and be philanthropic in some way and to support others who do the same

Socially Responsible Conditioning

We have been conditioned over time these past 25-30 years to prefer brands and corporations which do something to make the world a better place. To be honest, we don't even require too much accountability about what they are actually doing to make the world a better place (maybe that will come with time), but just the mere hint that they are "giving back," causes us to reach for their product, purchase their services, or refer them to others.

Giving back causes a company's profile to be elevated positively in the eyes of both the business community and the public. Socially responsible PR campaigns are big business for PR firms. Smaller companies without a large PR budget can benefit from crafting their own socially responsible messages as they interact with their clients and potential clients.

Have you given any thought to how you are positioning yourself or marketing your products and/or service? Do you let your customers, patients, clients, and referral sources know how your company gives back? Does your company give back? I guess that should have been my first question.

I'm so conditioned to expect it is being done, that I don't even suspect that maybe you are not doing it! If you are not doing something like this already, you are missing a great opportunity to create great buzz about you and your business!

Creating a "We First" Image

So, what are some strategies to keep in mind when you consider developing a "we first," as Simon Mainwaring puts it in his book by the same name, image? First of all, examine your personal passions.

There are certain aspects of what happens in our world that you feel very passionate about. For me, it's education. I remember so well when I was a young fourth grader and Mrs. Fielder had a very special corner of the classroom with her lending library set up. When we finished our seat work, we could quietly get up and go to that corner, select a book and sit on the comfy bean bag there and read while the rest of the class finished their assignment. Reading was a very rewarding, exciting and alive part of my life.

To consider that today many, many schools have closed their school libraries due to funding shortages, or that children in some areas of the world don't even have access to books at all, breaks my heart. Study after study has proven that reading contributes to academic success. Reading skills improve all your other skills—math, science, language, and even music. I am passionate about helping kids get a good foundation in literacy.

Maybe you are passionate about ending human slavery in our world, or saving the rain forest. Whatever your heart's passion is, get your fingertip on the pulse of what that is and why you feel the way you do about it.

Secondly, consider your corporate focus. What is it your company does--what service do you provide or what product do you sell? My company, BNI, focuses on changing the way the world does business. We've even trademarked that phrase! We teach small business owners and managers to collaborate and share referrals with as they build solid, deep relationships with each other based on mutual respect and cooperation. Our corporate philosophy is Givers Gain®. If I help you do well in business, you will help me do well and we will all succeed as a result! We want businesses around the world to grow as a result of more and more and more business people understanding this concept and practicing collaboration rather than competition.

We have truly started a movement with BNI. I cannot tell you just how gratifying it is to travel to all sorts of countries and hear, over and over, "I would not still be in business today if it were not for BNI and the support I have from my fellow BNI members." The concept of collaboration between businesses, rather than cut-throat competition, does not always seem to come naturally, but it is spreading, and I am absolutely thrilled with that!

Finally, find a way to bring the two focuses to a point of convergence. We realized within our first ten years of running BNI that a charity focus on children and education brought together my passion about education and my company's desire to see transformation in the world of small business. If we can have a positive impact on today's generation of kids, we are absolutely going to be preparing tomorrow's generation of business owners.

My company started a non-profit called the BNI Foundation with the motto "Improving tomorrow's business through education today." The BNI Foundation helps to provide struggling teachers, schools or other educational organizations around the world with the resources they need to offer quality education to kids. We do it in a way that is harmonious with our company focus and philosophy. Educators must be referred to us for consideration, because we want them to build a relationship with the local BNI chapters and members of those chapters so that they have advocates and supporters right in their own communities.

We have bought a lot of books through the years! We continue to forge strong relationships with educational programs like Junior Achievement, which is really working hard to provide our emerging business leaders with the experiences they need to become successful entrepreneurs.

Analyze your own personal passions and your business's focus. I would venture to say that you may find some harmonic resonance you had not considered. I have heard about shoe manufacturers who have started campaigns to help get donated footwear to countries where shoes are not readily available. I have heard about restaurant owners whose focus on a great restaurant experience has moved them to partner with non-profit organizations providing food to the undernourished and impoverished in their city. What about the spa and pool builder who donates a portion of each job to a charity dedicated to drilling fresh water wells in third world countries?

As you identify where your passion and your company focus intersect, remember to let your clientele know what it is you are doing to give back. Remember that the public wants to do business with a company which gives back. The consumer wants to purchase an item when proceeds from that purchase are going to help a cause they feel strongly about. It is interesting to consider that as I stood in front of that water cooler, it was the same brand of water which said "Health" that also said, "Education." I reached for the bottle labelled "Education." I wonder why?! You probably understand why now that you've read my story.

Ways to Give Back

You may be scratching your head at this point, thinking, "Just how am I supposed to 'give back'?" Your first thoughts may be to donate money to a cause, but donating money is not the only, nor is it always the best way, for you to give back. Sometimes it may be the easiest, but it doesn't have to begin there.

You can be as creative about giving back as you have time to be! I know one busy executive who is passionate about being socially responsible for whom signing a large check is not a big stretch, but who really wants to get in there and DO something beneficial in addition to contributing money. He makes the time to serve on a non-profit board. No matter how busy this man is, his heart is filled by being able to spend some of his time, which is really of more worth than his money, investing in his chosen cause.

So volunteering is one way to give of yourself and be socially responsible. There are ways to let your clients know what you are doing. Posting on your social media sites from time to time about your volunteerism is one way to be sure your clients are aware of your socially responsible involvement.

Another way to give back is to mentor others and share your expertise with them. Being in a mastermind group where you are all focused on helping each other achieve the successes you all seek can be a great way to serve others. There is a very successful artist in San Diego who purposely formed a mastermind group which meets weekly to provide support, inspiration and motivation in a small group format who understands that one of us is not as strong as all of us! He invited me to come from Los Angeles County to share from my book, Jesus and the Secret: Where the Word of God and the Law of Attraction Intersect, and I left wondering if I could overcome the distance (they are about 1 ½ hours South of me) to participate once a week--they were THAT dynamic! This is a man who is definitely giving back.

Joint Events

What about partnering with a non-profit whose cause is something you can really get behind to sponsor an event, an initiative or a drive for them? As I write this chapter, I have just been contacted by a BNI member not too far from me who is doing an online event and is willing to pledge 80% of the fees for the event to benefit the BNI Foundation! This kind of arrangement benefits his business because, not only will he be giving back to a cause he feels passionate about—children and education—but he will also be able to promote his event (and his business) through my social media sites and website. You better believe I will be telling everyone I can about his online event and driving traffic to him. At the same time, he will be giving my cause exposure to his clientele!

I know a couple who have become good friends of mine and my husband's who own an investment firm. We have co-hosted a webinar together which taught folks how to "Do Well by Doing Good." This cross pollinated both our businesses and was a tremendous amount of fun, as well. They also were co-sponsors of our large Spring fundraiser this year. We both benefited because our contact lists intersected that night at our party! Amazing things have happened as a result of that intersection. We both know different circles of folks and those people really enjoyed meeting each other. Deals are being done today because we did a joint event. Not only have we both personally and professionally benefited by our collaboration, but the ripples are continuing to flow outward to others who are benefiting from being part of this great, fun evening.

This firm has created a brochure especially for our charity which lets our prospective donors know how to use planned giving to benefit our cause. I have this brochure on my display table wherever I go. I am providing great information to my donors and I am also promoting their business, as they have the resources to help my donors utilize some of the vehicles available for giving to the BNI Foundation in a more powerful way.

These two examples illustrate how both parties can benefit when businesses work hand in hand with non-profits! The businesses are creating solid good will with their clients and their prospective clients and they are giving great exposure to our non-profit. The joint event we did with the investment firm brought in over $35,000 in donations—that reflects 35 teachers who are going to be able to receive a Givers Gain® Grant from the BNI Foundation!

Growing Your Business with Greater Visibility

A socially responsible image, a We First image, will help you grow your business in an exciting and fresh way. Examine your personal passions, your corporate focus and find that point of intersection between the two. Find a charity to which you can give, whether by donations, volunteering, or creating joint ventures, and let your clients and prospective clients know what you are up to in order to both create good will for your company AND to promote the charity you have chosen to support.

We live in a wonderful time when companies which are NOT socially responsible are the exception, not the rule. Learning how to harness the PR value of consciously contributing in a way that is coherent with your business's mission is vital. May you be blessed as you discover implement what that is for you!

Ideas & Actions on Giving Back

1. Look at ways in which your company could give back

2. Write down a list of charities or causes which are important to you personally

3. Set goals against the amount of time or money you want to give in the next 12 months

4. Come up with an idea for a joint event you could run locally

About the Contributing Author, Beth Misner

 Beth is an author, speaker, humanitarian, wife and mother, among many other things. Beth is the founder and director of the Journey Centre in Claremont, CA, a Christ-based centre for spirituality, healing and wholeness.

She holds a bachelor's degree in theology and master's degree in spiritual formation, which have equipped her for this aspect of her own life journey.

Beth lives happily with her husband, Ivan, in Claremont, California, and has three "young adult" children: Ashley, who is an accomplished artist; Cassandra, who is a college student; and Trey, who is also a college student. Beth, Ivan and Trey are black belts in karate and she practices and teaches T'ai Chi.

In order to give back to the community, as well as to teach her children the value and benefits of giving, Ivan and Beth started a non-profit charity in conjunction with their business, BNI. Through their work with the BNI-Misner Foundation, they are able to support children's educational programs all over the world.

Learn more about the BNI Foundation: http://BNIFoundation.org

Twitter: @BethMisner

Visit her website at: http://bethmisner.com

Download the Book "Jesus and the Secret": http://amzn.to/ZgkIYj

Chapter 8 - Giving Referrals

"Givers Gain® - The good you do comes back to you, over the long term and often in indirect ways." **Dr. Ivan Misner, Founder BNI**

Written By Contributing Author, Iain Whyte aka 'Big Man Talking'

This chapter is all about how to quickly instil confidence in people so they'll want to help you take your business forward. One of the best ways to do this is to learn the art of referral marketing. Giving referrals to others will instantly increase the amount of referrals you bring back into your business. Before you know how to give referrals you must first learn the fundamentals when it comes to generating them for your own business.

Why Focus on Referral Marketing?

There are numerous ways for you to get out there and generate new business, below is a list of some great ways for you to generate new clients:

1. Brochures
2. PR & News releases
3. Direct Mail
4. Writing Articles (offline and online)
5. Cold Calling
6. Advertising (in various forms)

The downside to these is that they are not always targeted, they might lead nowhere and can in some cases be expensive, time consuming and scary! When it comes to referrals, it's a different story. Referrals are the icing on the cake, they are very little hassle, have a high conversion rate, are low cost and are fantastic for increasing your business!

Here are some marketing success statistics. Say you send out 1000 mailshot letters (also known as direct mail or junk mail). It's best to buy a targeted list (from a list broker) or use your own client list. From this mailing, 10-20 people will typically sign up to your service or buy your product. In other words, you can expect a response rate of below 2%.

On the flip side, an enquiry from someone who's been referred to you typically gives an 80% success rate – and with little cost and effort on your part. People who are referred to you from someone they trust or respect, will already feel well-disposed towards you – and that's a state of mind you can't buy! Even if the product or service on offer isn't the cheapest the fact that it comes with a personal recommendation still increases the chances of the person being referred winning that business.

If you're in a forum or at a meeting and you explain that you need more information on something, there's usually someone who'll say,

'Hey, see this site! It's got everything you want. And there's more on site B and C too.'

Likewise, if you say you need a widget or service and ask if anyone can help you, you'll get 'Yes, try Boris; he's the man! Here are his details. I know he does his work well; he's not the cheapest but you can be confident it won't fall apart and the job will be done on time. Just mention my name when you contact him. In fact, shall I contact him and ask him to call you?'

In fact, because your contact has even included a 'negative' ('not the cheapest') it makes Boris and his offer seem more realistic. Plus your contact has added that despite the cost he'd use Boris because of his workmanship, so you're already halfway convinced even before you've met Boris. Even if you don't use him in the end, you may well still recommend him to others.

Now, if someone described you with the following words, wouldn't you be happy?

- Conscientious; Honourable; Gives good guarantees; Excellent value for money; Gets results; Good to work with; Explains things well; Finishes on time…

These are exactly the kind of words that referrers use about a business they know and trust. However, I must make this clear right now – referrals do require some work on your part!

1. Be Specific - you have to be clear what sort of clients you're looking for.

2. Helpful People - you must find willing people to recommend you to others.

3. Follow Up – always follow up with the new prospect.

4. Gratitude – always reward the person who gives the referral.

5. Give Feedback - give feedback and information to the referrer.

We'll look at each of these in more details now.

1. Be Specific

Imagine you're a personal trainer. You can tell me you want contacts from 'people who want to get fit'. Mmm, that's a bit difficult. I know lots of people who want to get fit, but who do you really want to speak to? Is it:

Jason – he wants to run the London Marathon next year.

John – he wants to cycle across the Pyrenees in the autumn.

Sahib – he wants to get up the stairs without puffing.

Sian – after having three children she's keen to get fit. Jeni – she wants to be able to walk a mile now she's recovering from her car accident.

Maybe none of those people are just what you want? I can't say. And I don't know if you'll visit them or expect them to come to you. I don't know the towns and villages in which you operate. I don't know how much you charge, and how often people should attend your sessions.

If you say: I want mothers who are finding it hard to get fit, and maybe feel put off at the thought of joining a gym. They probably feel they're wobbly in the wrong places, have lost some of their strength and balance, their clothes don't fit, they get puffed out easily, and have a poor self-image. Or they may just want to get out and be viewed as a person in their own right rather than someone's mummy. Their babies are old enough to be left with a child minder (I don't have crèche facilities). The mums need to have at least a couple of hours free a week and it will cost them £35 a session.

That's much closer! And you can get even more detailed if you want. If you then added stories of how you've helped some mums, showed some 'before' and 'after' pictures and testimonials and maybe a video of you in action, then that would really help. If you get a chance, you might even take some of us through a couple of your shorter diagnostic procedures and show us how our posture needs improving (and the knock-on effects and implications) or how we're not quite breathing correctly during exercise.

That'll help us to understand even more clearly what referrals you want. We'll be able to explain to friends and colleagues just what it is you're offering and how well you know your job.

Now, perhaps you want a wider range of clients as well as mums. If so, you'll have to be just as clear about their profiles. When you're trying to deliver the message in a hazelnut, a walnut or even a coconut, it's best to focus on just one client category at a time. If you get to speak for 10-20 minutes, perhaps you could cover three.

One more thing here – it helps to explain who you don't want as well. If you've asked for people who want to get fit and I send John (the would-be Pyrenees cyclist) to you but you have no idea about cycling, or no interest in the issues it creates, or the wrong facilities, then you will look silly, John will be annoyed, and I will feel peeved. Be clear. Be specific. It works.

2. Have Willing People to Help You Out

This is really useful! There are groups of people who are more likely to help you such as:

1. Those who have used and benefitted from your product or service.

2. Those you've helped with some of the giving activities in this book, remember 'Givers Gain'!

3. People you ask in such a way that they'd be pleased and proud to help you.

4. Those who know exactly what or who you're looking for.

5. People with a wide circle of friends, family, acquaintances and associates.

Now, it could be that the people in your network genuinely don't know any good business contacts for you but beneath every person you meet is a network of 500-1000 new contacts for you. I know lots of people: some are mums and some are married to mums, and some are single and fit young men. They in turn will know more people, and so on. Start the ball rolling.

3. Follow Up

As soon as you've been given details of a new prospect, or as soon as the prospect contacts you, follow up with them. Find out what they need and want at an early stage, so if you aren't the right person you can stop before anyone gets annoyed or offended. And if you know someone who can help the prospect instead of you, offer their details. They'll think you're great – and what could have been a negative becomes a positive.

Don't leave it a few days before you establish contact, as that will reflect badly on you and the referrer. If you're going to be out of the office, leave a message on your answer phone and set up an email auto-responder message. Say when you'll return and that if they leave their details you'll contact them as soon as possible after you get back.

4. Reward the Referral Giver

As you will have read in Chapter 4, it's all about giving gratitude. Ignore this bit at your peril! If you don't thank people in an appropriate way, you'll come across as ill-mannered, ignorant, selfish and as someone who doesn't value others' contributions. I know an accountant who regularly referred people to a solicitor. He told me one day he was going to stop doing it. 'Why's that?' I asked. He replied that the solicitor had made a lot of money through these referrals. My accountant friend wasn't complaining about the solicitor making money. The problem was, he never said thank you and not once did he reciprocate.

Sometimes a referral doesn't end up in more sales for you, but you can still thank your referrer for trying. Properly thanked, your contacts are far more likely to try to find you more referrals. What's more, others will notice your efforts and feel good about you too – which in turn may lead to more referrals.

5. Keep the Referral Giver Informed

It's not only polite to thank a referrer for their efforts, but it also pays to give follow-up news. This can work in two ways. The first is that if the referrer got the wrong end of the stick, it's now time to come clean. That way, any potential awkwardness between any of the parties involved can be neatly nipped in the bud. It's important to sort out any misunderstandings quickly and in a friendly fashion. Also ask each other how you may help in another way.

The second way of giving follow-up feedback is this: when you tell your referrer exactly how you were able to help and the benefits you delivered to the person they referred, then that referrer has learned even more about your business and what makes a great referral for you. This means their next referrals will be even better targeted.

And of course, the referrer will be pleased you've taken the time to feedback what happened as a result of their efforts. Even better, they'll know that the person they referred you to will be feeling good about them: brownie points all round!

Confidence & Referrals

Confidence and referrals go hand in hand. You need to have confidence in your own business to generate referrals and ask for them, and you need to have confidence in other people if you are going to refer them by giving referrals.

Here's a question every business owner should answer: "What's the purpose of your business?". Most will reply, 'To acquire and keep profitable clients.' In other words, you're in business to make profits. Even if you run a charity, you've got to make more money than you spend.

If people lack confidence in you, they won't tell other people about you (unless they're telling them to stay away from your business, and you really don't want that). Let's take a quick look at why people might not have confidence in you and your business:

- Someone's been telling bad stories about you

- They weren't really sure what they wanted and even after speaking to you they're still unsure.

- Your goods or services are shoddy.

- You haven't delivered on time.

- You're charging more than you said you would.

- The buyer lacks confidence in themselves or their decisions. Or maybe things are bad in their life right now and they're suppressing the thoughts, and they're projecting their insecurities or anger onto you.

- You lack confidence in yourself / your service / your product, and it shows.

Confidence can be a strange and nebulous thing. But you can gain confidence in yourself and in what you offer to others. By building your own confidence, you can build your prospects' and clients' confidence in you. If people have confidence in you they'll both buy from you and pass your name on to other people. Brilliant! So confidence can equal referrals. And if you act on them promptly, referrals are the best kind of business you can get.

Confidence = Referrals = Sales

People who are referred to you are more likely to use your products or services than those who come across you by chance. So referrals are critical to the future success of your business. People I coach often say at this point, 'Yeah, but...':

- 'Yebbut I don't know enough people who have the right contacts.'

- 'Yebbut I'm shy.'

- 'Yebbut what happens if they don't like my product?'

- 'Yebbut, Yebbut, Yebbut, Yebbut...'

In fact, people often think that it's really hard to find others who'll refer work to them regularly. But is it? Maybe the ideal referral source for you is nearer than you think. However, before I show you that, I'd better dispel those Yebbuts quoted above!

'Yebbut I don't know enough people who have the right contacts': How do you know that? If you're sure, then do something about it. I have a friend who loves networking. She discovers a lot about her contacts by asking the right questions, listening to them, and remembering what they've said or writing it down. She also finds out about who her contacts know and who their contacts are? When she needed to ask someone a technical aspect of her website, for example, she asked a few friends. Since building websites wasn't really their thing they didn't know what she was talking about, but she was given a name of someone who could help.

This friend asks a lot of people about a lot of things. She has enough self-confidence that she's not afraid of people knowing she doesn't have all the answers. And she realises that people like to help rather than laugh at her ignorance (or what I like to call 'temporary un- knowledge'. It sounds kinder).

It's actually very easy to find people to ask. Just join networking groups, and then learn to mingle, ask and listen. The groups might meet in person like BNI, Women's Networks, the Chamber of Commerce and various other networking groups, or they might be online, individuals communicating through webinars and online forums, LinkedIn for example. If you cannot find a local networking group locally, then why not start one up?

'Yebbut, I'm shy'

Lots of people are – and often you wouldn't know it to look at them. You can go on courses to help you overcome shyness, get help to conquer it (counselling, CBT2, TFT3, NLP4, etc.), and actually attend networking events. It's amazing how easy networking can be: just ask people about themselves, their businesses and their needs. And show you're listening. People will really warm to you. Ask what you can do to help the person you're talking to. You'll find when you're helping someone towards a solution, the words flow more easily and you begin to smile without trying.

Here's a golden rule: don't cling to the first person who speaks to you! Ask them (for example) if they know someone who can help you find a good printer for your stationery. If they do, ask them to introduce you. Ask people for their business cards, and offer yours in return. Make sure that your cards clearly show the benefits you offer. Your new acquaintances may well pass them on saying, 'I don't really know that much about Julie's product, but she seems very genuine: why don't you give her a call?'

'Yebbut, what happens if they don't like my product?'

Depends why! If your product is shoddy, then you have no right anyway to be putting someone in an awkward position. Change your product and then ask again. Sometimes it's not so much that someone dislikes your product, it's simply that they don't like that product in general – or don't need it at that time. Me, I don't like golf, so I'm not going to be interested in your golf stuff. However, just because someone doesn't like or need your product doesn't mean they won't pass your name on.

So while I might not like golf, I do know plenty of avid golfers. And if your state-of-the-art new club will swipe 16 strokes off their total, then I'll definitely tell them about you and you will get referrals.

'Yebbut, Yebbut, Yebbut, Yebbut …'

Maybe you're just a 'glass half-empty' person, or maybe you're just in the wrong business. Work out whether you're in your particular business because you want to be, or because you feel you should be, or because someone else wants you to be. Find your passion and work with that.

If it's just one part of your business that bothers you (for me, its book- keeping and filing), then outsource that part. Don't use excuses to stop you growing your business; you'll be getting in your own way.

Target Market Commonality

One of the easiest things you can do to make giving referrals easier for you is to find people who have Target Market Commonality with you. This is essentially, groups of business people who share the same types of clients and offer different products and services. You can join forces, swap clients easily, form a common bond and make sales from each other's clients. These can often be referred to as Referral Partners or Strategic Alliances.

For instance, you might be a web designer. Get together with graphic designers and copywriters so you can target start-up businesses, those who want to move into online sales, or others whose web presence is currently weak, dodgy or positively gruesome. If you're a solicitor wanting to talk to non-English nationals who are setting up businesses in the UK, you might want to know an accountant, someone who writes in plain English, a printer, a translator, and so on. Why would you look for a group or groups with target market commonality? The main benefits are that as you build up trust among your group members, you can:

- Give more business to others
- Get more business in return
- Feel more confident about yourself
- Ask for and receive more referrals
- Feel a lot less lonely in business

Take the time here to identify your target market commonality group or the types of people you'd like to approach and get to know them, and then ask for referrals to them. Once you know where they network you will find it much easier to give referrals to others. So, we've now seen that because we have a lot of target market commonality with a great many people, there are many people who are potentially good referrers for our businesses.

However, to maximise the number of referrals we get and cause an energy shift in our 'client conveyor belt', it's absolutely critical that we target, approach, cultivate and execute the right relationships in the right way. This is where 'The Five Fundamentals of Referrals' come in.

The 'Five Fundamentals of Referrals'

We've explored how confidence and referrals go hand in hand. Now we'll look at five main concepts in more depth. We'll look at how to motivate by giving; how to instil confidence in others; how to educate others as to what you want; how to keep disciplined; and how to find the right referral partners.

- Motivate through 'Givers Gain'
- Instil confidence.
- Educate others on who and how.
- Stay disciplined.
- Find the right referral partners.

1. Motivate through 'Givers Gain'

Givers Gain® is the philosophy of the world's largest and most successful networking organisation in the world, BNI (Business Network International). This is an organisation I have been involved with for over 11 years. Givers Gain works on the basis that if you help other people to get more business, they will help you generate more business in return. At the time of writing this book, BNI exists in over 50 countries around the world and has tens of thousands of members all working together with Givers Gain at the heart of everything they do, and with good reason. It's one of the most powerful tenets of business.

If you're just in business with a view to making profits and blow all else, then you run the risk of having a lonely time – and you'll be much less likely to get referrals. It's a widely held belief that people manifest their thoughts and feelings – call it karma, putting out the vibes, the Law of Attraction – whatever. It all amounts to the same thing. If you're good to people, you'll benefit. Maybe not immediately, but sometime, when you need it, it'll come back to you.

For instance, one business friend of mine was always there to help others. She didn't do it with reward in mind; she just likes people and enjoys sharing her knowledge. At one BNI meeting she stood up to speak about her business, and she hesitated. People began to smile as she could usually be relied on to do something humorous, and then they realised she was quite upset. She explained her major client had just pulled out without any warning: 'Yes, I know, I shouldn't have relied so much on having work from just one source, but the owner was a good friend. I'd have expected some notice! But anyway, I don't have enough work at all. I need help, please.'

The group rallied around her, some offering support, a couple offering loans, and several phoning through with referrals that week. Her work level was soon back on track as was her self-confidence. One of the best ways to motivate others to take action is to give. So her focus on giving referrals to others, meant that she got the support and help she needed instantly.

2. Instil confidence

We've established that to generate referrals you need confidence. You must have confidence in your service or product and you should be seen to have confidence. Others need to share that confidence and they must know that your promises will be kept. When they feel you are offering a sound service, they may pass your name on. I say 'may' because nothing is guaranteed. It helps if they like you and if they know who/what you're looking for. So how can you help instil confidence within yourself and others? We'll start with you, and then look at how you can spread the 'message'. I'm assuming here you're running your own business, or maybe working on a commission basis for someone else.

First, you must believe in your product or service. Would you buy it? If not, why not? Maybe it's because you have no need of it right now: in that case would you buy it for a member of your family or a close friend? Can you honestly say that your product is better than someone else's? If you can't, do you make up for the shortfall by offering it at a reduced rate to a different set of buyers? If you are trying to get away with promoting something as better than it is, it'll show. For those who work on commission it really, really helps to believe that what you're selling will benefit your potential buyers. If you don't, get out now! You have plenty of transferable skills, and many businesses require good sales people.

When people ask you about your product or service, don't launch into a feature-laden explanation, and don't go on about your business ('we were established in 1994, blah, drone, blah') unless they specifically ask. Instead, talk enthusiastically about how your product has helped your clients or customers. Find out why the enquirer has bothered to ask you, and give your answer in a way that draws their situation (or their friend's) into your reply. You can also display your confidence by advertising, dealing politely and efficiently with complaints and returns, and by giving guarantees.

If you consistently advertise your product or service, people will assume that (a) you believe in it, and (b) it must be good and profitable otherwise you wouldn't keep advertising, and (c) they'll feel comfortable because they recognise your name and know you're not a fly-by-night business. Be up-front too about how you would deal with an unsure prospect or an unhappy customer. If you're seen to have a good guarantee and a non-fussy returns policy, people will have more confidence in referring you to others. If you fight your corner over something that others perceive as a minor issue (even if you are convinced you're in the right), negative word will spread.

Unless it's really worth fighting over, be as gracious as possible. You can even go a bit further: 'I'm sorry this wasn't what you needed. Please accept a refund and this bouquet of flowers for your trouble.' That sort of word will travel too. The last bit of confidence comes in people knowing exactly what your products or services offer, and who they need to talk to about you. Let them know. This leads us nicely onto...

3. Educate Who? And How?

If you want to generate referrals for your business, you need to be specific, give examples, tell stories, and repeat. Of course you also need to find people to educate, especially those who understand business and how to find prospects for you. What I'm saying is, just chatting at a social event may get you some referrals, but belonging to business groups can get you a whole lot more.

Many networking groups give you a chance to 'pitch your wares' either within a formal structure or as you circulate and chat with other members. What happens is, you get a period of time to promote your offer and to ask for the referrals or introductions you want. If you want to generate referrals for your business you need to have a clear focus on who your target market is, tell great stories about how you help your clients, instil confidence in your business and share what makes you totally unique (like the questions explored in the chapter in this book on Giving Meetings). When you do attend networking events, always listen to what other people are looking for. If you can help them in some way with their referral requests you will stand a much better chance of growing your own business through referrals.

4. Stay Disciplined

This section is short, but no less important. Basically, the message is: Stay disciplined, and keep on track. It's easy to let slip one time and then it's even easier to slip further again and again. Don't give up – keep at it. People like repetition and familiarity. They want to see you there and they want reinforcement of your message, your needs and your trustworthiness. Besides, it might take time before they see an opportunity to help you. If times are tough, stay disciplined. If times are good, stay disciplined.

5. Find the Right Referral Partners

This is very important. Firstly, it helps to use referral partners who can deliver the goods, and secondly you need to trust them. You are only going to give referrals to people you know, like and trust, in the same way that people are only going to refer you if they know, like and trust you also.

Find people in professions or categories that you know you would be able to give referrals to if you built up a strong relationship. Some examples are below of the kind of referral partners for various industries:

Profession:	Good Referral Partners:
Photographer	Jeweller, Travel Agent, Videographer, Bridal Shop, Wedding Planner
Plumber	Builder, Electrician, Roofer, Plasterer, Architect, Engineer
Recruitment	Human Resources Consultant, Business Coach, Accountant, Printer, Training Company
Accountant	Solicitor, Financial Advisor, Bank Manager, Business Coach
Web Designer	Copywriter, Marketing Agency, Graphic Designer, Printer, Promotional Products

Think about what type of referral partners would be right for your business. Then start researching them.

- Look in your existing contact list of people you know for them
- Go through your mobile phone contacts
- Go to LinkedIn and use the 'Advanced Search' feature
- Use Google to simply search your location and their profession
- Ask your best business contacts if they know a good [insert profession]

Once you have identified them go and have a giving meeting (see Chapter 3). Meet with all sorts of business people and friends to find out who knows people in the categories you have identified. You will be surprised that once you know who you want to talk to, and start asking others for help you will see dramatic results in your business. Make sure that you either like or admire the people you ask to meet with. Remember that you'll need to feel comfortable asking for or receiving a referral from them.

By now you will have read Chapter 2 in this e-book on 'Giving Goals'. Imagine what would happen if you decided to start focusing on giving referrals to others. For example you decide to give one referral on average per week for the next year. That's a lot of giving activity; imagine how powerful that level of giving would be in terms of the results back to you. By finding strong referral partners with target market commonality you will find it much easier to give referrals and work with people who you can build a strong strategic alliance with to help you grow your business.

Actions & Ideas on Giving Referrals

1. Find local networking groups to visit and see which of them suits you best. Find a group of people in business that you can get to know and start giving referrals to.

2. Go to training on referral marketing or read lots of books on referral marketing (I suggest you start with those written by Dr. Ivan Misner).

3. Write down a list of at least 5 referral partner professions that if you were to meet with could start giving referrals to you, and of course you could give referrals to.

4. Set your giving goals for the number of referrals you will give in the coming 12 months.

About Contributing Author, Iain Whyte

 Iain is better known as 'Big Man Talking', he is respected for his positive attitude, business insight and unfailing ability to motivate and inspire audiences across the world, Iain is a dynamic, engaging and enlightening speaker. He has WOWED audiences internationally with his unique style and fantastic content.

Iain is Author of "Life, Business & Speedboats", a practical book on networking and referral marketing which gives you all the tools you need to learn more about how to grow your business by tapping into the people you already know. Iain has spent 11 years as a highly experienced Director with BNI and now works with clients to help them achieve their business and personal goals as a business coach and mentor.

Iain's purpose and passion in life is to have a positive effect on the lives of others. Iain speaks across the world, and has addressed business owners and entrepreneurs in the USA, Australia, Malaysia, Sweden, Ireland, and the UK.

Iain was born and raised in Aberdeen, Scotland. He now lives in central Scotland with wife Val, daughters Morag and Heather and son Angus. A family man, with a big heart and a real passion for helping others, so much so that his proudest achievement was winning a highly respected 'Givers Gain' award in Los Angeles at the International Conference of BNI in 2004.

Want to follow Iain or read more from him, click on the below links to learn more:

More books by Iain Whyte: http://amzn.to/ZeV9cq

Visit Iain's website at: http://bigmantalking.com

Follow Big Man Talking on Twitter: @iwhyte

Become a Fan on Facebook: http://facebook.com/bigmantalking

LinkedIn: http://www.linkedin.com/in/iainwhyte

Chapter 9 - Giving Online

"Think of giving not as a duty but as a privilege."
John D. Rockefeller, Jr.

Written by Sam Rathling & Contributing Author, Rick Itzkowich

Many of the techniques and strategies in this book can be used in relationship building and face to face situations with people in your network. However it can be very easy to transfer your acts of giving into an online situation.

Why LinkedIn?

If you are not on LinkedIn and you are running a business, then before you read any more of this book, go and set up a profile on LinkedIn. Click on this link to sign up for free: http://linkedin.com.

If you are already on LinkedIn but are not currently getting business from LinkedIn then hopefully this chapter will reveal some great giving tips that will help you to secure more opportunities.

I was an early adopter of LinkedIn, I joined in 2003 as a Recruitment Consultant and to date have access to over 20 million profiles through my extended LinkedIn network. Every time I run a search for a person or a company, I am usually connected in some way through my extended online network and that helps me to grow my business. I have over 45 recommendations from people giving social proof that I am great at what I do and my profile appears in search results between 80-100 times per day, and is viewed in excess of

800 times per month. I regularly secure new clients through LinkedIn.

Here are some statistics that might compel you to want to take action when it comes to LinkedIn:

- In 2012, LinkedIn reached a milestone of over 200million members in over 200 countries, many of the decision makers that you are looking to target for your business are on LinkedIn (both SME's and large corporates)

- In 2012 over 5.7 billion searches took place for people and services that they offer – if your business is not on LinkedIn then you are missing opportunities!

Why else would you want to be on LinkedIn?

- You can optimise your LinkedIn profile to appear at the top of LinkedIn and Google searches for your niche

- You can join up to 50 groups on LinkedIn, where your target market are networking online

- Many of the features on LinkedIn are free to use for your personal profile

- You can create a Company profile page

- You can use LinkedIn to generate leads and business opportunities for you and your company

- You can link your LinkedIn updates to Twitter and position yourself as an expert in your field through updates

- It is the world's number one online business platform, and your competitors are already there!

I have asked Rick Itzkowich, also known as "The LinkedIn Guy" to contribute to this Chapter, to share his expertise on how you can apply the principle of Giver's Gain® to the world of online networking via LinkedIn. Rick and I met in early 2012, in Bangalore of all places.

You'll hear more about my trip to India in Chapter 15. I was fortunate enough to share a stage with Rick at a large business networking conference, and I saw Rick deliver an amazing presentation to over 600 Indian based Entrepreneurs about LinkedIn.

We have since stayed in touch and now help each other's business to grow as referral partners for each other. I asked Rick to share his top tips on the use the 'Givers Gain' philosophy with LinkedIn.

Rick and I both train companies and business owners on how to get the most out of LinkedIn, it would take us off topic if we were to use this chapter to train you on how to use LinkedIn for business. We have handpicked a few free resources for you to learn more:

Free LinkedIn Resources

The author of "How to Really Use LinkedIn" is giving away 1 million free copies of their LinkedIn book which you can download here. You simply need to provide your name and email address to get your copy (this really is giving in action):

http://www.how-to-really-use-linkedin.com/

Rick's blog and Twitter feed @thelinkedinguy are also great free resources for learning more about LinkedIn:

http://www.rickitzkowich.com

I regularly write about LinkedIn on my Sam Rathling blog, a few articles you may like are listed below:

For tips on your Professional Headline:
http://www.samrathling.com/linkedin-professional-headline-tips/

For tips on building your reputation on LinkedIn you might like:

http://www.samrathling.com/how-to-build-your-online-reputation-via-linkedin/

http://www.samrathling.com/how-to-improve-online-reputation-with-linkedin-part-2/

Here are 17 of the best free LinkedIn Articles I could find, just for you, some great resources here for Company Pages, Endorsements and Profile Writing:

http://www.samrathling.com/tips-for-linkedin/

If you need help with your LinkedIn profile then why not buy a gig for just $5.00, at http://Fiverr.com where people are willing to help you out with LinkedIn for a very low cost.

If you would prefer professional video tutorials then Rick's series of videos would secure a very strong recommendation from me. Well worth it if you are starting out and currently getting zero business from LinkedIn.

Rick's 8 Top Tips for Givers Gain® on LinkedIn:

1. Always respond positively to invitations to connect.

2. Make sure to respond to direct messages sent to you.

3. Write recommendations for people in your network.

4. Share useful content.

5. Be a connector and introduce people to each other.

6. Offer encouragement when someone shares something they're excited about.

7. Share your knowledge freely with others.

8. Actively promote others through your status updates and/ or group discussions.

So getting back to our main topic of Giving Online, I asked Rick to share the best example of giving or 'Givers Gain' that he has ever seen on LinkedIn. This next section was written by Rick:

I recently received the following message from one of my LinkedIn connections who is a Travel Agent specializing in cruises. I really enjoyed this as an example of Givers Gain® on LinkedIn:

Example Givers Gain Message on LinkedIn

Subject: Connection Highlights — How can I help you?

Hi Rick,

How is your summer going? I hope you're managing to stay cool. I've noticed that the leaves are starting to fall already, so perhaps we'll have an early winter.

This summer I took a trip to Italy and a MSC Mediterranean cruise with my family. We had a great time. Rome was just amazing with ruins right next to new buildings all over the city. The highlights of the cruise for me were Tunisia (totally different culture) and Pompeii.

Once again, I would like to highlight selected people in my network that I know personally can offer real value, helping you to offer a new benefit to those people in your network.

If you are looking for something specific yourself, please let me know. Conversely, if you would like to get the word out about a product or service that you offer, I would love to hear more about it.

I am proud to say that I know personally that these associates can help make the lives better of those that you like, know and trust. Please take a look at the recommendations below to see if you know someone who could use this service. If you do, kindly introduce us.

If this is something you would rather not participate in, please let me know, and I won't send these highlights to you.

A friend of mine recently had his last several tax returns reviewed by my Accountant. He did the happy dance in the elevator after meeting with her, because he was going to be getting $557,000 back from the IRS, which was 1/3 of his annual income! If you have a friend who would like their taxes reviewed to see if they are owed money, let me know, and I'll put them in touch with her.

Who do you know that has a new teen driver in the family? They may want an insurance company that helps inexperienced drivers develop safe driving habits through their safety education program.

Hope to hear from you soon.

From Name

[End of Message]

Analysis of this Giving Example on LinkedIn

Let's analyze my connection's message in relation to the 'Givers Gain' philosophy. Look at the subject line – *"How can I help you?"*. First of all, it immediately grabs my attention. Then she has included a friendly, personal short paragraph that serves to remind me of what her business is -- without directly mentioning it.

Next she goes on to explain how I can add value (give) to those in my network. She also asks me if I need something else, OR if I would like to get the word out to her network about MY products or services. She respectfully offers me a way to opt-out of her messages. And, last but not least, she highlights two of the people in her network.

She truly has taken the time to help others, as well as she offers to help me – all through our connection on LinkedIn – the foremost business networking social media platform.

Why Giving Online is Important

Giving online is very important because it helps you stand out from the thousands of people who are using social media to pitch and sell their products or services. It helps you establish the VCP process® – first gaining Visibility, then earning Credibility and lastly enjoying Profitability.

I am sure you've received the follow up connection email that goes something like this – "Wow, not that we've connected, it'd be great if we met for coffee to discuss this great new product that my company has just come out with. In fact if you do take 30 minutes to talk with me, I'll be able to offer you a 30% discount on your first order." This strategy doesn't come close to incorporating the 'Givers Gain' philosophy. It screams – me, me, me.

One of the ways I use the 'Givers Gain' philosophy is that as soon as someone either invites me to connect or accepts my invitation, I respond to them with a polite and congenial thank you message. This message also includes an invitation to receive a gift from me. This gift is the opportunity for them to receive QuoteActions – a series of email-based inspirational quotes and actions designed to provide an uplifting message on a regular basis.

You can learn more about QuoteActions here: http://quoteactions.com.

I get tremendous response from this offer because it truly is a gift – because it is unrelated to my core business. This last point is very important. I often get "gifts" that are nothing but discounted offers in disguise for a product or service. I don't perceive these as gifts, but rather as marketing offers. Nothing wrong with that – just don't offer them to me as a gift.

Please understand that when I offer my gift, it really doesn't matter to me if the person accepts it or not. I do get a fair number of people that accept and a number that decline my gift. Those that choose to decline still write back and tell me they appreciated the kind gesture. And, that's the whole point. With the immediate thank you message after connecting on LinkedIn, you start positioning yourself as someone who understands how to build and nurture relationships -- and that type of giving is very important. It builds your social capital.

Building relationships requires dialogue. The invitation to connect gets the dialogue started. Unfortunately most people stop the conversation once they accept. With my 'Givers Gain' approach, you keep the conversation going. You put "the ball in their court" so to speak. It's now up to them to respond and keep the conversation going with me.

Giving & LinkedIn Groups

If you want to grow your LinkedIn network and referrals, you need to provide your insights and thought leadership in relevant groups where your target market is active. This doesn't mean bombarding groups with redundant content and constant links back to your website. Those tactics make you look like a spammer. They can result in getting you ignored, deleted and/or blocked from the group.

Instead, use your groups as opportunities to learn more about your target market and share insights. Strive to become a valuable resource and contributor to the community–and viewed as a subject-matter expert in your field.

Say you are an Accountant/CPA you may have a handy itemised deductions explanation sheet in PDF format. Make it available as a download for your connections in the group to use – let them private label it for their clients. Or as a public relations expert you might provide a list of 100 news topics for people to use as a reference for PR planning.

Another way is to engage in the conversations, supporting people with their comments. Reinforce the feedback given by others in the group – you help increase their credibility. When you edify others and serve as a team player in a group – it's definitely using the 'Givers Gain' mindset.

To summarise, LinkedIn is THE professional business online networking site. There's no better place to practice 'Givers Gain' than on this powerful portal. If you have any success stories, share them with others. Spread the word about using LinkedIn to build and nurture profitable relationships.

Most of this chapter has focused on LinkedIn, however there is nothing stopping you from applying the same techniques to all of your other social media activities.

A few simple tips are:

Giving on Twitter – Tips for Success

1. Use the Follow Friday hashtag #FF on Friday's to recognise people who follow you, promote others to your followers

2. Always thank someone who re-tweets one of your tweets. Eg. @samrathling Thanks for the RT!

3. Be seen to be giving relevant content to your followers by sharing great tips, quotes and articles.

4. Make the ratio of great content for others vs. self-promotion about 9:1. Keep selling to a minimum.

5. Mention others in tweets to recommend services of people in your network

6. Thank people and practice giving gratitude on Twitter

Giving on Facebook – Tips for Success

1. Choose one day each week to theme as a 'Thank You' day, where you choose one of your Facebook Fans and thank them for supporting your business and add a link to their website or Facebook Page

2. Promote other people via recommendations and testimonials on Facebook

3. Actively talk about other people in your network on Facebook to give them visibility to your Fans

4. Share great content and useful articles that other people will like and enjoy

5. Whenever you meet someone for a giving meeting, mention them in your Status Updates

Hopefully you will have seen from this chapter that the giving process can continue throughout all of your marketing efforts both online and offline. The key to success with giving online is to always think, how can I help others, and not how can I sell to others. Once you have a giving mindset and apply it to your online efforts you will really see some great results and more giving from others coming back to highlight you and your business.

Actions & Ideas on Giving Online

1. Create a 'Thank You' theme on your Facebook Page or LinkedIn updates, mention a business owner each week and highlight their business to your Facebook Fans or LinkedIn Connections to give them greater visibility.

2. Share 1 Article per day with your network that will help them, follow relevant news in your industry

3. Give a person connected to you on LinkedIn a recommendation

4. Mention 1 person on Twitter every week for the next month, with a link to that person's website or blog

About Contributing Author, Rick Itzkowich

Rick I, the 'The LinkedIn Guy!' is an international Speaker, Trainer & Entrepreneur. Rick is a genuine people connector. He understands and practices networking like few others do. As a successful entrepreneur, Rick creates turnkey products, like Link Power, QuoteActions and new Yikes! Business Networking Workshops.

These unique tools meet today's need for tactics to increase your business. His informative and entertaining live presentations, along with workshops, articles, interviews, podcasts and blog messages on adding strategic networking strategies to a company's marketing plan are in high demand. Rick speaks to a diverse group of organizations, and he is a regular SCORE workshop presenter.

Internationally Rick earned the Best Speaker Award at the "You Learn Twit Face" international social media conference held in Dubai. Rick's 2012 speaking engagements took him back to Dubai with stops in the UK and India. Most recently he launched his Yikes! Workshop world tour in San Diego and Houston. Rick frequently serves as a subject-matter expert resource for both online and offline social marketing reporters and bloggers. Feel free to connect with Rick on LinkedIn!

Links for Rick Itzkowich:

Email: rick@rickitzkowich.com
LinkedIn: http://www.linkedin.com/in/ritzkowich
Twitter: @thelinkedinguy

Rick's Facebook Pages:

http://www.facebook.com/rickitzkowich

http://www.facebook.com/YikesWorkshop

Rick's Websites

http://www.rickitzkowich.com

http://www.quoteactions.com

http://www.yikesworkshop.com

Chapter 10 - Giving Testimonials

"No one has ever become poor by giving." **Anne Frank**

What is a Testimonial?

A testimonial is a review (generally very positive – but genuinely so) of a product or service that is displayed on the sales pages, in emails, and even inside of the product being sold. These are a big help to the customer who wants to hear from real people how the product/service helped them out. It helps them make up their mind to buy or not.

Every business loves testimonials from happy customers. Why? Because they give social proof that your business is worth spending money with. One of the best books you could invest in is "Influence" by Robert Cialdini.

He explores 6 key factors in influence and the chapter on Social Proof demonstrates why such a big emphasis should be placed on gaining social proof for your business.

So you know that it is important to get great testimonials from clients you have done business with, however this book is all about giving.

Giving testimonials to other people is a really great way to give you extra publicity and free advertising, in addition, because you are giving them to other people and helping their business to grow you will gain back from the business you recommend either directly or indirectly.

Why Give Testimonials?

- Giving a great testimonial to another business instils confidence in the products or services of the person receiving

- If you give one to someone else, they will be inclined to return the favour and give one back to you

- The person receiving the testimonial can use it in their everyday business to win more clients

- If written in the right way, you can indirectly promote your own business through the testimonial. The likelihood is that it will be included in somebody else's marketing materials and online. Imagine your name, website, picture, and comments being displayed on the sales letter for a top product, it is free advertising!

- It makes you feel great, giving a testimonial is a really nice thing to do and can lift your spirits too

- You can gain attention from a potential target client - Provide a great testimonial, and you'll get noticed by the product or business owner, even if they don't include it right away on their website. This can be the start of a longer term relationship that can lead to referral partnerships, reciprocal promotion, or becoming a more extensive case study for that product which will lead to even more exposure.

Formats You Can Use To Give Testimonials

The way in which you give a testimonial or recommendation can vary and they can come in a range of formats. The following is a list of formats you could choose to use:

- Written Testimonial

- Verbal Testimonial

- Video Testimonial

- Social Media Endorsement eg. a Tweet, mention on Facebook etc.

- LinkedIn Recommendation (see chapter on Giving Online)

- Blog or Article about the product or service

The way in which you give the testimonial can affect the leverage it gives you back in return. All testimonials are good to give, however the most effective ones from this list would be written, video and LinkedIn recommendation. These three types of testimonials give you much greater visibility than the other formats.

Different Types of Testimonials

When giving a testimonial, it is important to write a good one so that it gets seen by more people and delights the business owner enough to want to use it more in their marketing materials. So if you are stuck, here are some great lines and examples you can use in the testimonials that you give.

Type 1: Before and After

Briefly give the background before using the product. Typically, you'll identify a major pain, confusion, or doubt you had about succeeding or reaching a goal. Next explain what happened immediately after you experienced the product or service. Explain in the after part what you accomplished after applying the product or service over a period of time (usually a month or more).

Type 2: Overcoming and Objection

This is where you give a testimonial that directly answers an objection a person would typically have about buying a product. Common objections are not having enough time, not having enough money, it won't work for me, etc. Say for example that you wanted to do a testimonial for a company who help people with their social media, and you know that a common objection about Twitter and Facebook is people think they are a big waste of time. You might create your great testimonial about how before learning the lessons by [Insert Company], you thought social networks were a big waste of time. But once you were taught the strategic methods inside the social media course you attended, you now know how to spend just 10-15 minutes a day to build stronger relationships with your growing "tribe" of followers who are now your raving fans and ambassadors.

Type 3: Monetary, Time or Transformation

The second type of great testimonial is one where a major change occurred, where the change happened quickly and measurably. This could be a monetary, time, or body transformation that is easy to describe or demonstrate. For example you saved 34% on your insurance, you got back 10 hours a week by using a product or system, or you lost 16lbs in weight after 3 months etc.

Giving great testimonials is not just about saying how much you loved a product or service. It has to be written in such a way to persuade a reader to buy, because they recognise something about you in them. By doing this you'll find those readers won't just gravitate towards the products, they'll gravitate towards you as well which could also lead you to more business.

Format for Giving a Written Testimonial

A great written testimonial should always be given on your own headed paper. When you present the testimonial to another person, you should also place it into a frame. There is a great reason for doing this. Imagine you received a written testimonial from a client in a gorgeous frame. What would you do with it? The chances are that you would firstly be delighted and tell lots of people about it, but also place it on the wall in a place where everyone can see it!

Expect this to happen to any written testimonials you give to others, free advertising! But first you need to know a good structure for writing a written testimonial so that you increase the chances of it being placed on the wall of someone else's office for everyone to see.

[YOUR HEADED PAPER]

Dear [Insert First Name],

RE: Testimonial for [Insert Company Name]

Paragraph 1 - Summary of the situation, your business, the problem you or the person you referred were looking to solve or why you were in need of the particular service or product.

Paragraph 2 – How the fellow member helped you or the person you referred. What did they do that was unique? What was particularly outstanding? How did this compare to other similar companies you had used in the past? How was the problem solved?

Paragraph 3 – Insert one of the three types of testimonials here (1. Before & After; 2. Overcoming Objection; 3. Time, Money or Transformation). What results have been delivered? What has happened AFTER the business has been done? Use phrases such as...Since using Company X we have seen... our profits rise / our time significantly reduced / our processes improved etc.

Final Paragraph – Recommendation & Thank You - I would have no hesitation in recommending Company X to any business looking to... I would like to thank you and your team for the excellent work you have completed and look forward to building a long term relationship.

Kind regards

[Insert Your Name]

[Insert Your Title]

Why not think about someone you know in your network that has done a brilliant job for you. You have probably been meaning to get around to writing them a recommendation anyway, and hopefully this chapter has inspired you to give a great testimonial to them. Giving testimonials can become a great habit that not only gives you greater visibility, but also makes you feel great too. They are a very powerful tool but somehow many of us are just too busy to give them. It's up to you whether you integrate this strategy into your business and I know those of you that do will gain massively.

Actions & Ideas on Giving Testimonials:

1. Think of at least 5 people that you could give a testimonial to and write them on a list

2. Using the structure given in this chapter, write and give a written testimonial to the people on the list

3. Give a LinkedIn recommendation to someone you have been meaning to for a long time

4. Record a video testimonial for a business contact who you really want to motivate to refer your business

Chapter 11 - Giving Responsibility

"It's about giving employees permission & encouraging them to just be themselves" **Tony Hsieh CEO Zappos**

Written by Contributing Author, Julia Foerster

Before you get into this chapter, I want to personally introduce you to the author who has contributed this chapter and also Chapter 14. Julia Foerster has been a part of my life for over 6 years and today is someone who I respect, appreciate dearly and admire for her ambition, drive, attention to detail, loyalty and commitment to me and my business. She is truly brilliant and I know you will learn a lot from her contributions to this book.

Our adventure together started when she interviewed for a role in my company having just arrived in Ireland from Germany back in 2007. She was impressive in interview all those years ago, and has impressed me ever since, Julia has proven to be the best hire I have ever made. Finding your equivalent of Julia could be the key to unlocking your business growth.

The reason I have asked Julia to write two chapters in this book is that she is living and breathing proof that giving responsibility to your team and making sure that their happiness is the heart of all you do as a business owner can motivate, engage, develop and retain the best people you have. If you want your business to grow then the strategies that Julia writes about in relation to giving responsibility and happiness can free you up to take your business to new heights, allowing you to focus on the right activities.

Julia is now the Operations Manager in my recruitment business, and I invited her to contribute to this book, writing from her personal experience in working for me. She will show you the power of letting go, delegating, growing your team and keeping that team happy and engaged. She is an expert in talent management, staff motivation, employee engagement and retention strategies. After all she has been on the receiving end of my giving activity in these areas ever since I took on my first employee. So now I'll hand this chapter over to Julia...

My Story

At Recruitment Magic, it is all about staff happiness and giving responsibility. I have had the absolute fortune to meet Sam at the start of my professional career in Ireland 6 years ago and needless to say, it has been amazing ride working with her. At the time, I was looking for an opportunity to hit the ground running and apply my existing skill-set obtained during my M.A studies at university and while working in several different part-time roles covering the fields of administration, marketing and customer service.

One of the main reasons I am still working with Sam is her incredible ability to share responsibility and provide endless opportunities for professional development, personal growth, and continuous learning while discovering new talents in me that I did not even know existed!

Every single time I have asked to be given more responsibility, I have received it with no questions asked and that has definitely increased my attachment, commitment, loyalty and dedication to Sam and her business. The positive, high-energy, vision and value-focused work environment has fuelled my enthusiasm and motivation in everything I do and I am happy about the professional and personal autonomy and independence I have achieved as a result of working with Sam. At the same time, this has enabled Sam to free up her time to build a new business and spend more time with her family. I am extremely honoured and proud to be able to say that I am now managing the recruitment business on Sam's behalf and that I have recently become her business partner as a shareholder in the company.

Look After your People & the Business Will Look After Itself.

Employees are the major asset of any organisation and retaining positive and motivated staff is vital to overall business success. Employees that enjoy what they do and the atmosphere in which they work in are more likely to remain employed with their company and thus contribute more effectively to your overall business success. However, one of the greatest challenges facing employers today is finding and keeping talented, high potential employees, and in the current scenario almost all leading organizations are facing problems of employee retention.

There are several reasons as to why an employee decides to move on, and they can range from monetary dissatisfaction, to a negative environment at the workplace, internal politics, complicated hierarchies, lack of challenging work, to poor supervision and lack of effective coaching and management.

So what happens to your business when key staff members become dissatisfied and demotivated?

- Boost in Absenteeism

- Increase in employee turnover

- Potential Poaching from Competitors

- High Recruitment & Training Costs

- Potential Loss of Internal Confidential Information

- Negative Effect on Workforce Morale

- Decrease in Productivity

- Low Job Performance

- Negative Company Image

- Damaged Client & Supplier Relationships

- Loss of key skills, knowledge and experience

- Damaged Reputation

- Negative Impact on Customer Service

Retaining positive and motivated staff will help you manage employee turnover and develop a stable workforce with a high morale, saving you considerable money on replacement, hiring and training costs, while maintaining high productivity & profitability, and overall job performance. If your employees are engaged and happy, they will be less likely to join one of your competitors, or talk negatively about your business. To the contrary, they will become advocates of the company and its products and services and act as an ambassador of the organisation because they are proud in what they do, contributing to the bottom line business success.

The longer employees stay with your company, the more emotionally attached they are and this enables them to develop a sense of loyalty towards their workplace in a competitive environment. Employees who are focused, serious and committed and care whether the company is performing well will strive hard to live up to the expectations of internal management and will take ownership of their work. They will perform better and will be more motivated. Thus, strategies that target employee engagement should be one of the primary measures of the long term health, success and vitality of your business. Can you think of a Fortune 500 company that reached success without top performing people who have grown and developed over time with the company?

Empowering and engaging staff is not only vital to help create a positive, high energy work environment and strengthen an employee's commitment to the organization, it helps you focus on business critical aspects, ensuring on-going customer satisfaction and product & service sales, enhancing client relationships, contributing to internal process improvement, developing effective succession planning, and solidifying deeply imbedded organizational knowledge and learning. It saves you costly candidate searches, as well as time and money invested in recruitment & selection efforts, and training.

But why do some companies act in ways that so frequently encourage high potential employees to quit their jobs for a better opportunity? Organisations that believe in increasing employee engagement levels concentrate on the following areas:

Culture

In order to successfully engage employees you need to develop a strong sense of leadership, vision, values, effective communication, as well as a strategic plan and HR policies that are focused on the employee. Retaining good staff begins during the recruitment phase, with a strong job description and the sourcing & selection of a candidate who will successfully fill the role and stay long-term

Commitment & Cooperation

Organisational commitment and positive working relationships will foster a willingness of individuals working in a team to pull in the same direction and achieve overall organisational goals

Responsibility

Refers to feeling empowered. Employees who feel empowered have a sense of belonging and excitement about their jobs, they feel engaged at an emotional level and are willing to give their best all the time. Response - ability describes the ability to respond and thus becoming answerable and accountable for something within one's own power, control, or management.

This chapter describes some effective employee retention strategies that involve giving responsibility to help you engage your employees, getting them attached, involved and committed to your business by increasing their responsibility and scope of work. If you are able to increase the responsibility of your staff, then you can start to delegate tasks to your team which can free you up to actually focus **on** the business instead of constantly feeling like you are **in** the business and unable to get the time to do the tasks that you know you should be doing as the business owner.

The first step is to understand what employees want and how to facilitate employee engagement. Once employees are engaged they will be more than happy to take on extra responsibilities. Here are some areas for you to think about in relation to your team if you have one.

If you already have a team or are about to embark on hiring staff to grow your business then it is time to consider exactly what it is that employees want so that you can ensure the longevity of their time with you.

What Do Employees Want?

Clarity of Job Expectations

A satisfied employee knows clearly what is expected of them every single day and works within a specific framework of success. Changing expectations creates unhealthy stress and can make the employee feel unsuccessful in their assigned job. Ask your employees: Do you know what is expected of you? Once the ideal candidate is hired, orientation and on-boarding is paramount. Clearly define job responsibilities and accountabilities, and provide a clear understanding of the role and performance targets necessary to complete the role successfully. This instils confidence and reliability.

Perception of Job Importance

Great employees do not just want to enjoy their work, they want to be passionate about it. Employees insist on knowing how their specific jobs fit into the grand scheme of things and what they can do to help the organisation get to where it wants to go. Why is what they do important to the company? What are the expectations of the customer?

If you want your employees to feel valued and inspire their passion on your behalf, encourage them to make their own decisions. Let them use their enthusiasm, creativity and hard work to implement ideas. An employee's attitude toward the job's importance has the greatest impact on loyalty and customer service.

Happy Working Environment

Create and maintain a workplace that attracts, retains and nourishes good people. This covers a host of issues, ranging from developing a corporate mission, culture and value system, insisting on a safe working environment, to creating an enjoyable physical work space and developing clear, logical and consistent operating policies and procedures. The overall goal is to make your company a place where people *want* to come to work. You will learn more about this in the upcoming chapter 'Chapter 14 - Giving Happiness'.

Positive Company Culture

Employees want to know that their values fit in with the company's overall mission. They want to know where the company is going and what it will look like in the future. Do you have a values statement that clarifies and supports a culture of openness? How is the company doing financially? Where does it stand in the marketplace? Clarify your mission, create a values statement, and communicate positive feelings. Find out if your employees *really* know the vision, mission and values of your company.

Ask them why they work for you. You can then use that information to recruit new employees, saying: "Here's why people work for us. If you value these things, perhaps you ought to work for us, too." Does the employee feel that managers and colleagues "walk the talk" in terms of the company's values?

Effective Internal Communication Systems

Employees want a culture of openness and shared information and the more information you give people about what they are doing, what the company is about and why you do things the way you do, the more valuable it becomes. Help people to understand all the nuances of their jobs. If you operate in an open environment where managers share information, you can expect reduced turnover rates.

To assess your culture's level of openness, ask questions such as: Do your employees know how the company is doing in key areas such as sales, financials, strategy and marketing? Do you give performance feedback on a regular basis or only at annual review time? Do you encourage individuals and departments to share information with each other?

A Feeling of Being Valued

Many people don't feel personally valued and respected, and they believe that no one would miss them if they were gone from the business. Your staff members must feel rewarded, recognized and appreciated. When people don't feel engaged, all the money in the world can't hold them. Listen to your employees when they have a concern, a question or a contribution to make. Say thank you and reward hard work with bonuses and gifts because they make the thank you even more appreciated.

Ask yourself: Does the employee feel that his efforts are being recognised and valued? Do employees get to make a difference in your business? When people buy into your clearly stated corporate values and have the information they need to get the job done, they tend to stick around.

Consistent Support System

People want to do a good job and they want to excel and nothing can be more frustrating to an employee than a lack of training or the proper tools to successfully complete his or her duties. Remove obstacles and barriers to getting the job done, and provide moral and mental support. If an employee fails at work, ask yourself the W. Edwards Deming question, "What about the work system, is causing the person to fail?".

Provide the tools, time and training necessary employees need to be successful - it shows a commitment and investment in that employee and will encourage the team member to stay with the organization. Ask yourself: Do you see employees as valuable resources that make the company go? Does the employee feel supported by his line manager and colleagues?

Quality of Supervision

In many cases, employees leave their position because of their supervisor or manager and a lack of clarity about expectations, about earning potential, a lack of feedback about their performance, a failure to hold scheduled meetings, and a failure to provide a framework within which the employee perceives he can succeed. If your supervisors have the knowledge, training and sensitivity to work effectively with people on an individual level, you will get the commitment and attachment you need to retain employees.

Nurturing staff based on clear and open communication should be a day-to-day, on-going activity. Nothing communicates respect and empowerment more than actively listening to your employees because being heard builds self-esteem and trust. Appreciate their input, concern and feelings. People work for people not companies, so it is important that their voices are being heard and their concerns addressed.

Opportunities for Career Advancement/Improvement

Employees are not always looking for a promotion, but they need opportunities for advancement. Personal and professional growth and improvement constitutes a very strong driver in today's workforce. Give people *productive* work to do and provide challenges. Encourage people to take initiative and recognise and reward creativity and innovation. Does the employee want to stay with the company and develop their career?

Provide opportunities for professional development and growth for team members to acquire new skills and knowledge useful to the organization. If an employee appears to be bored or burned out in a current position offer to train this individual in another facet of the organization where he or she would be a good fit. Help employees balance company goals with their personal goals to get them focused.

Continuous Training and Education

Good employees want to develop new knowledge and skills in order to improve their value in the marketplace and enhance their own self-esteem. However, don't just "throw" education and training at your people in a random fashion. Instead, organise and structure your training so that it makes sense for the company and the individuals who work for you. Take time to explore your employees' different needs and the best way to meet those needs. Establish a learning culture in your organization and create individual learning plans that include in-house skills training and development and bringing experts in to educate employees about subjects that affect their personal lives. Encourage people to join professional and trade associations. Invest in career planning. Provide incentives for learning. Take advantage of internet learning (podcasts). Operate a corporate mentoring programme.

Regular Feedback from Managers and Supervisors

Feedback is the key to giving employees a sense of where they're going, but many organizations are remarkably bad at giving it. Sometimes all employees want to hear is Thanks. You did a good job. Do not wait for an annual performance review or evaluation to give feedback on how an employee is performing. Shortening the feedback loop will help to keep performance levels high and will reinforce positive behaviour.

Giving regular feedback does not necessarily need to be scheduled or highly structured; simply stopping by a team member's desk and letting them know they are doing a good job on a current assignment can improve employee morale and increase retention.

Quality of Working Relationships with Colleagues

If employees' relationship with their managers or colleagues is damaged, then no amount of money or reward will persuade the employees to perform at top levels. Management must take the time to get to know team members. The greatest complaints that employees express after leaving a company is a feeling that management did not know or cared they existed. It is crucial that managers and supervisors take the time get to know the team members who work under them.

Learn and remember a team member's name, what skills and talents they bring to the table, and what their business interests are. The time spent by management getting to know team members is well invested and can eliminate having to continually hire and re-train new employees.

Competitive Compensation (Monetary)

Employees want to feel that they are being paid appropriately and fairly for the work they do. Discuss total employee compensation (salary, benefits, bonuses, health insurance, pension, training, stock options etc.). Use flexible employee benefits to respond to a changing workforce. Be sure to research what other companies and organizations are offering in terms of salary and benefits.

You can be sure that if your compensation package is not competitive, team members will find this out and look for employers who are willing to offer more competitive compensation packages. If you decide to give raises to individual employees, stay competitive within your market sector, geography and position, and be fair. Did the staff person deserve the raises? The perception of fairness and equitable treatment is important in employee retention.

Adequate Compensation (non-monetary)

People want fair compensation, but contrary to most managers' beliefs, money rarely comes first when deciding whether to stay or go. The majority of workers look at non-monetary reasons first. Offer time off, flexible working hours, Job-Sharing, Home Office Space, sabbaticals, Special projects, Committee involvement, public acknowledgement, career development and training, and other forms of non-financial employee compensation.

Provide childcare and/or eldercare and employee assistance programmes. Arrange for company organized discounts on company and client purchases and professional services, and fund fitness-club memberships. Support Community and Charity involvement. Smart employers use a variety of hard (monetary) and soft (non-monetary) employee compensation strategies to make it difficult for other companies to steal their people away.

You can learn how to give great recognition to your team in the next chapter - Chapter 12 – Giving Recognition.

Reward Systems

Design reward systems to stimulate employee involvement. An incentive to reward good work is a tried and test way of boosting staff morale and enhancing engagement. When people exceed expectations, give them a bonus but ensure your incentive scheme hits the mark with your workforce such as: Setting realistic targets, selecting the right rewards for your incentive programme, communicating the scheme effectively and frequently, have lots of winners and reward all achievers, encouraging sustained effort, present awards publicly and evaluate the incentive scheme regularly. Today, more and more companies pay for performance – in every position, not just sales.

The Ability to Provide Input

Everybody has opinions and ideas, and some are better than others. However every team member wants to feel that their input is welcome and will be taken seriously without ridicule or condescension. Some of the greatest ideas can come from the most unlikely of places and people. Creating a culture where input is welcome from all level of the organizational chart will help your organization grow and encourage long term employee retention. Plan regular brainstorming sessions as part of your team meeting.

Once you have the information about why people work for you, ask: "What can we do to make things even better around here?" Do it in a positive way and listen closely to what your employees say. Out of these conversations will come many good ideas, not only for improving conditions for your employees but for all facets of your business.

Team Engagement

Use behavioural style assessment tools, such as Insights, Myers-Briggs or DISC, to help people better understand themselves and each other and communicate more effectively with each other. Help employees to set life goals and get focused on where they want to go.

Then help them to see how their goals match up with company goals and that they can achieve their goals by staying with the company. If people believe they can achieve their goals and objectives by working in your organisation, they will think twice before going somewhere else to work.

Scope of Responsibility

Make use of a team member's talents, skills, and abilities. A motivated employee wants to utilise their talents and skills and contribute to work areas outside of his specific job description. This can also provide work variety and helps to break up the everyday grind of work. Adjust jobs to fit strengths, abilities and talents.

Ask yourself this question. How many people in your business could contribute far more than they currently do?

Utilising a team member's talents in areas other than their current position will indicate to an employee that management appreciates and recognises all that an employee has to offer to the business. Avoid micro-management and reduce reporting requirements.

Balance Work and Personal Life

When possible, offer job flexibility to encourage a healthy work-life balance. Family is incredibly important to your team members. When work begins to put a significant strain on one's family no amount of money will keep an employee around. Stress the importance of balancing work and one's personal life.

Small gestures such as allowing a team member to take an extended lunch once a week to attend a doctor's appointment or run important errands or attend a family member's soccer game or school play will likely be repaid with loyalty and extended employment with an organisation.

We will cover this more in Chapter 14 – Giving Happiness.

Manage Overtime

Ensure that you staff the business adequately to reduce the amount of unwanted overtime a team member must work. Some employees enjoy the extra money that accompanies overtime hours, while others would rather spend their time with their families or doing other activities they enjoy. Burnout can be a leading cause of turnover. Recognise the warning signs and give employees a break when they need it.

Keep the Door Open

There are a lot of employees out there that would like to return to a previous company they worked for. These 'Boomerang' employees are usually very committed to their position and the company and therefore can become the some of your best recruiters for new talent and mentors for existing employees. The time they have spent away from your business has given them the additional knowledge of the market, and they have personally experienced that perhaps the grass isn't greener on the other side.

Many business owners still believe that salary dictates people's employment decisions. But for the most part, people want opportunities to grow and learn, to advance in their careers and to work on challenging and interesting projects. They want to be recognised and appreciated for their efforts and they want to feel a part of something that adds value to their community.

Your best employees, those employees you want to retain, seek frequent opportunities to learn and grow in their careers, knowledge and skill. Without the opportunity to try new opportunities, sit on challenging committees, attend seminars and read and discuss books, they feel they will stagnate. A career-oriented, valued employee must experience growth opportunities within your business.

How to Retain Your Staff

Take a look at your team in your own business. Are you doing your best to retain your top talent? The book "First, Break All the Rules" by Marcus Buckingham and Curt Coffman and provides 12 fundamental questions that employees ask of themselves, that great managers / leaders need to answer if they hope to keep their employees motivated and engaged. Regular reflection on these questions provides the answers on how to best lead your team.

The 12 questions employees ask, and need positive answers to, are:

1. Do I know what is expected of me at work?

Do my team members have clear job descriptions, and clarity around projects, tasks and expectations).

2. Do I have the materials and equipment I need to do my work right?

Have they got the resources they need to succeed in their role?

3. Do I have the opportunity to do what I do best every day?

Do you have people in the right jobs, where they can use and build on their strengths?)

4. In the last 7 days, have I received recognition or praise for doing good work?

When was the last time you gave praise to the individuals in your team? If it wasn't in the last week, it's not regular enough. People crave recognition - your role as leader is to encourage and cheer-lead your team.

5. Does my supervisor or someone at work seem to care about me as a person?

Do you know who your team members are as people, not employees?

6. Is there someone at work who encourages my development?

Do you provide opportunities for your staff to learn new skills and feel like they are moving forward?)

7. At work, do my opinions seem to count?

People leave managers, not jobs. What structure do you have in place for your team members to provide their feedback? And do you listen when it's given?

8. Does the mission / purpose of my company make me feel my job is important?

Do your team members know how their role fits into the bigger picture?)

9. Are my co-workers committed to doing quality work?

Are you letting poor performers set the standard or are you encouraging people to lift the bar? The standard your walk past is the standard you set. Good performers can be demoralised if poor standards are accepted in others.

10. Do I have a best friend at work?

Are you providing opportunities for your team to grow supportive relationships at work? Work is a big part of their lives, so it's vital for people to have fun and friendship.

11. In the last 6 months, has someone talked to me about my progress?

Are you providing regular reviews and feedback to help people with a sense of direction at work?

12. This last year, have I had the opportunity at work to learn and grow?

Are you providing opportunities for advancement?

This is a great list of questions, and one which I have used in my own role managing teams. This can really help you to focus on your best asset, your people. Take some time and seriously evaluate what you are doing in your business to encourage the retention of high potential employees.

Having a seasoned and well trained workforce can deliver a competitive advantage that is difficult to replicate with any other measures. The best part is that most of your efforts to retain your employees come free or with little cost, compare this to the cost of losing your key people and take action today to give more responsibility to those who you know want to see your business grow and succeed.

The 'It's Quicker If I Do It Myself' Syndrome

One of the main reasons that most businesses do not grow, is that the business owner cannot let go, fails to delegate and cannot give responsibility of main tasks to others. Regardless of whether you have staff or not, delegation of key tasks to employees and/or freelancers is still a critical skill to master. Many business owners have what I call the "it's quicker if I do it myself" syndrome. You know that someone else could do it, but for the time it would take you to show someone else or train another person in how to do it, it would be much faster for you to do it, so you battle on and continue doing mundane tasks, that do nothing to grow your business.

It's time to stop, sit back and really start to look at what tasks you could give to others. If you have a team they will love the increased responsibility and if you don't have staff then you can always use sites such as http://fiverr.com or http://elance.com to hire people at low cost to carry out tasks for you.

How To Start Giving Responsibility To Others

1. Make a list of all of the tasks that you currently do yourself in your business, and I mean EVERYTHING! Take each daily and weekly activity and write it down, no matter how small. This works best using a whiteboard or large flipchart paper. Lock yourself away in a room without distractions when you do this.

3. Next allocate a specific amount of time to each of the tasks you have listed out. By doing this you will be able to see exactly how much time you could free up for yourself to focus ON the business, by getting rid of tasks that are not helping your business to grow.

2. Use the **K.A.D.E** system to work out how you divide your tasks. Write next to each task the following letters:

K – Keep

A – Automate

D – Delegate

E - Eliminate

Let's look at each of these in more detail:

K = KEEP

These are tasks that you must keep doing yourself, these are not tasks you can delegate out to others and should only include activities which are directly going to impact the growth of your business. These tasks should include strategic planning, sales and business development, high value client management etc. The main tasks that you keep in this exercise, should be activities that build your sales pipeline. If you are not spending time on direct selling activity or indirect selling activity then your business growth will be much slower.

A = AUTOMATE

Could you automate the task using technology? Could you put systems or templates in place that will automate regular tasks in your business that would save you and/or your team a huge amount of time. Even if you are not sure how you would automate it, but you think there could be a way to automate it, then mark it with an A for now.

D = DELEGATE

It is likely that this list will be the longest when you do this exercise. There are bound to be numerous everyday tasks that you currently do that could be delegated. Don't worry about who, at this stage, the point of this exercise is to show you just how much stuff you could give to someone else. If you want some ideas, then take a look on Fiverr.com and Elance.com and go shopping for people that could help you with tasks. You can outsource practically any aspect of your business and for a lower cost than you might think (starting from just $5.00!). If you cannot afford to take on staff at the moment, you could also consider getting an intern.

Internships can be a great way to give, you give experience to young, ambitious student looking for work experience and you give them responsibility for tasks you no longer want to do yourself. In our business we have taken in over 25 interns, some have since gone on to secure permanent employment with us. Interns are free, fully insured if you use the right company to source them and if you get a good one, they can add massive value to you as a business owner, especially when it comes to delegation.

E = ELIMINATE

These are tasks that you have maybe been doing out of habit that really are no longer necessary. These are tasks that would not be missed if they did not continue to get done. These are tasks that you have been spending time on that are not ultimately producing any tangible results.

Now go through the list of eliminate, delegate and automate to add up the total amount of time you would save each week or each month if you took steps to give responsibility to others and free up your time.

You may think that it might be quicker to do it yourself in the short term, but in the long run you are only hindering the growth of your business. You should only keep the tasks that you enjoy and that you are good at, otherwise you will procrastinate and begin to resent your business because of the time it is taking you away from your family and friends. Once you start to get used to giving responsibility to others you will probably find that other people actually do a better job than you anyway.

Once you give responsibility to others, empower and engage your team and free up your time to focus on what really matters, with effective delegation you will never look back.

Actions & Ideas on Giving Responsibility

1. Take a look at your current team members, decide who could and would be in a position to take on more responsibility from you.

2. Do the K.A.D.E exercise to look at what you can keep, automate, delegate or eliminate.

3. Start delegating more tasks to your team members.

4. Go shopping on Fiverr.com and Elance.com and see who you could find to help you with tasks in your business.

About Contributing Author, Julia Foerster

 Julia currently works as the Operations Manager of Recruitment Magic, the home of low-cost online recruitment advertising campaigns, serving clients across the UK & Ireland. As a key member of the team and a shareholder in this business, Julia and Sam have been working together since 2007. Without Julia, Sam would not have been able to grow her businesses and achieve the work/life balance that she now enjoys as an Author, Trainer and Speaker.

Julia is a dedicated BNI member and Director Consultant, helping members of BNI in Ireland South & West to grow their businesses through networking, word of mouth and referral marketing. In 2012, Julia was nominated as BNI Director Consultant of the Year, shortlisted from over 400 BNI Directors in 40 regions across the UK & Ireland.

Originally from Germany, Julia moved to Ireland in 2007 to be closer to her sister, her niece and nephews. She now lives in Cork City and enjoys a variety of different activities such as going to the theatre, dancing and music. Julia is extremely talented, born to parents who are both heavily involved in music. She has played the Cello since the age of 10 and has studied piano and singing, and is currently an active member of the Cork School of Music Fleischmann Choir.

Julia is passionate about travelling, as you will have seen from her contributions in this book. Her favourite trip was in 2011 and 2012 when she was given a sabbatical to take a round the world trip for 4 months. She is currently training to become a Life & Career Coach, studying for this in her weekends and evenings. She loves to write and blogs for the Recruitment Magic business and has contributed two Chapters to this book.

You can learn more about Julia here:

Connect with Julia on LinkedIn:
http://www.linkedin.com/in/juliafoerster

Follow Julia and the Recruitment Magic team on Twitter:
@Recruit_Magic

Become a fan of Recruitment Magic on Facebook:
http://facebook.com/RecruitmentMagic

Visit the Recruitment Magic website: http://recruitmentmagic.com

Chapter 12 - Giving Recognition

"Giving credit where credit is due is a very rewarding habit to form. Its rewards are inestimable." **Loretta Young**

Most employee development happens on the job. This development comes from the new learning opportunities that you provide to your employees, as well as the chance to gain new skills and experience in an organization. Few employees are satisfied with going nowhere. Most hope to learn more, to be involved in higher-level decisions, and to progress in both responsibility and compensation. Giving your employees new opportunities to perform, learn, and grow is therefore very motivating. It shows your employees that you trust and respect them and that you have their best interests at heart.

You aren't going to motivate your employees by building a fire under them. Instead, find ways to build a fire within them to make work a place where your employees want and are able to do their best. Here are some simple ideas for you to be able to give recognition to your team both inside and outside of the office environment:

Giving Recognition within Your Office Environment

Here are some ideas for you to recognise your team within the office:

- Create a Hall of Fame wall with photos of outstanding employees.

- Nominate an Employee of the Month and award them for top performance.
- Give a handwritten thank you note, or make a thank-you card by hand.
- Bring an employee bagged lunches for a week.
- Cover the person's desk with balloons.
- Inscribe a favourite book as a gift.
- Swap a task with an employee for a day – only it's their choice which task.
- Give the person a copy of the latest best-selling management or business book.
- Give special assignments to people who show initiative.
- If your team is under pressure, bring a bag of marbles to work and take a break to have a contest.
- Include an employee in a "special" meeting.
- Create an Above and Beyond the Call of Duty (ABCD) Award.
- Start an employee suggestion program.
- Smile. It's contagious.

Ideas for Giving Recognition Outside of Your Office Environment

- Plan a surprise picnic on a sunny day and take your team out for the afternoon.

- Encourage and recognise staff who pursue continuing education by sending them on an external training course.

- Wash the employee's car in the car park, or arrange to get their car valeted.

- Serve ice cream outside of the office to all of your employees at the end of a project.

- Have an annual "Staff Appreciation Day" where the management team supply, cook and serve food.

- Send flowers to an employee's home as a thank you.

- Plan a surprise achievement celebration for an employee or group of employees.

- Recognize employee's personal needs and challenges outside of the office.

- Express an interest in employee's career development goals.

- Encourage employees to participate in community volunteer efforts.

- Treat an employee by taking them out to lunch.

- Home bake a gift (cookies, bread, etc.) for an outstanding employee or team.

Giving Recognition in Other Ways

There are many other ways for you to give recognition to your team, for example:

Give Employees Interesting Work

Although some of the tasks that you personally perform day in and day out may have long ago become routine for you, these very same tasks may be very exciting and challenging for your staff. When your employees excel at their assignments, reward them by delegating some of your duties to them or by designing interesting projects for them to work on. It doesn't cost you anything, and your employees will be stimulated at the same time that they develop their work skills. Your employees win, and your organisation wins, too.

Give Employees Increased Visibility

Everyone wants to be recognised and appreciated for doing a good job. One of the easiest and most effective ways to reward your employees for no cost is to recognise them publicly for their efforts. You can gain visibility for your employees' efforts by announcing their accomplishments in staff meetings, sending out e-mail messages that congratulate your employees for their fine work with copies to all the other employees in business.

If your company is bigger and has an internal newsletter you can submit articles about your employees' efforts to the company newsletter, and many other similar approaches. Give it a try. What have you got to lose? This technique is free, easy, and very effective.

Give Unexpected Time Off

Another great, low-cost way to reward your employees is to give them some time off. In today's busy business world, time off from work has become an increasingly valuable commodity. People want to spend more time with their friends and families and less time in the office. Of course, the effect of downsizing and reengineering has been to give everyone more work to do, not less.

Whether you give an hour off or a day off, your employees will be pleased to be able to get away from the office for a short while to take care of personal business or just relax. They will return refreshed from the time off and grateful for the recognition that you gave for their efforts. Send them home early by surprise or tell them not to come in tomorrow. This will have a massive impact on their commitment to you and ensure that they are fully engaged in their work and in turn your business will grow.

Give Employees Information

Your employees crave information. However, some managers and business owners hoard information and guard it as though they were in charge of all the gold in Fort Knox. Instead of withholding information from your team, share it with them. Fill them in on how the company is doing and what kinds of things are in store for the future both for the business as a whole and for your team.

By giving your employees information, you not only empower them with the tools that they need to make more informed and better decisions, but you also demonstrate that you value them as people. Isn't that what everyone wants? Giving information to them through verbal and written communication is key to growing your business.

Give Feedback on Performance

Employees want more than ever to know how they are doing in their jobs. The only one who can really tell them how they are doing is you, their manager. Ask them to join you for lunch or to have a beer. Ask them how things are going and whether they have any questions or need help with their work. Provide them with feedback on their performance both formally and informally.

Thank them for doing a good job. You don't have to wait until your employees' annual performance review to give them feedback. Indeed, the more feedback you give your employees, and the more often you give it, the better able they are to respond to your needs and to the needs of your business.

Give Involvement in Decisions

Involve employees especially in decisions that affect them. Doing so shows your employees that you respect their opinion, and it also ensures that you get the best input possible in the decision-making process. Employees who are closest to a work process or a customer are often in the best position to see the best solution when a problem arises.

Your employees know what works and what doesn't perhaps even better than you do. Unfortunately, many staff are never asked for their opinion, or if they are, their opinions are quickly discarded. As you involve other employees, you increase their commitment to your business and at the same time help to ease the implementation of a new idea or organisational change. The cost is zero and the pay-off is huge!

Give Independence

Employees highly value being given the latitude to perform their work the way they see fit. No one likes a supervisor or manager who always hovers over employees' shoulders, reminding them of the exact way something should be done and correcting them every time they make a slight deviation.

When you tell employees what you want done, provide them with the necessary training, and then give them the room to decide how they get their work done, you increase the likelihood that they will perform to your expectations or even above expectations. Not only that, but independent employees bring additional ideas, energy, and initiative to their jobs, too. Independence equals motivation and a motivated and fully engaged team member will always add massive value to any business.

Give Flexibility

All employees appreciate having flexibility in their jobs. Although some jobs, such as receptionists, retail staff, and security guards, clearly require strict schedules and work locations, many other jobs such as computer programmers, technical writers, financial analysts, for example, aren't so tied to the clock or your established workplace.

Giving your employees flexibility in determining their own work hours and their own workplace can be very motivating to them. In companies where giving employees this much flexibility is not possible, you can still empower your employees with the authority to make day-to-day decisions about exactly how they perform their work or how they respond to customer service issues.

There are so many ways that you can give recognition, which ideas you choose and the level of recognition you give is entirely up to you. But before you move on from this chapter, think about this... if tomorrow morning your best member of staff gave you their notice and told you they were leaving in 4-12 weeks, would your business be able to grow and achieve all of the goals you set out to achieve this year? Would you be able to get someone just as good for the same money, fully trained up before they left? What extra time would you have to give their area of the business while you replace them? What would be the real cost of not being able to recruit someone into their role fast?

If the thought of any key team member in your business leaving the company fills you with dread, then start increasing the amount of recognition you are giving to your team to ensure that a supplier, head-hunter, client or commission hungry recruiter doesn't snap them up and leave you with a big unexpected problem to solve. If a team member is motivated, happy and given recognition from you they are much less likely to consider going and in turn you will be more likely to grow your business.

Actions & Ideas on Giving Recognition

1. Choose three of the ideas from the list of ways you could recognise a team member or all of your team and decide when you will implement them

2. Write down the consequences of a key member of staff leaving, and devise a recognition based strategy to motivate and engage them more in their work

3. Plan a team away day which is partly fun and partly business related, involve the team in some brainstorming and idea generation activity so that they feel involved in decision making as well as feeling highly valued. Use this as an opportunity to communicate where you want the business to go and where they fit into that vision to get their commitment and buy-in to your business growth.

Chapter 13 - Giving Connections

"The most basic and powerful way to connect to another person is to listen. Just listen. Perhaps the most important thing we give each other is our attention..." **Rachel Naomi Remen**

I almost called this chapter 'Giving Relationships', until I started doing some research on Amazon for books like this one that focus on giving. When it comes to giving and relationships, I can tell you now that most of the books that show up when you run a search on giving are more about giving of a...let's say, sexual nature so I'll leave it up to you to only imagine the kind of book titles that come up! They are certainly not the kind of book titles you would expect to see when it comes to business books so I decided to change this chapter to 'Giving Connections', but I did find it funny though.

One of the best stories I know about receiving a brilliant connection happened in the UK to a fellow BNI Director, Paul Cameron. I am sure you in your business dream about landing big clients and dream introductions, well Paul has not one but two great stories about introductions he was looking to land and one of them was to one of the most well-known Entrepreneurs on the planet, Sir Richard Branson.

Paul's story demonstrates the power of referral marketing as he not only gained Elton John as a client through a connection, but he also received a direct referral to Richard Branson through BNI. *Paul's Story is taken from an article he wrote about this incredible connection:*

"In November 2011, I participated in a charity cycle ride from Angkor to Saigon. While taking a break from the trek and sightseeing on November 20th, I received a phone call. I considered ignoring the call, but instead took it. It was Elton John looking for a special first birthday present for his son, Zachary, who was born Christmas Day 2010.

He had heard about Treehouse Life (my company) and our customized tree houses and asked if we could build and deliver one by his son's special day. My answer, of course, was yes. We just needed to work through the design and contract.

By the following Saturday, we had the design confirmed. When asked how he heard about Treehouse Life, Sir Elton John said he received a referral from Gary Barlow, for whom we had completed a treehouse project over a year ago. In the two weeks prior to leaving for Cambodia, I had attended the Phil Berg workshop on the power of "6 Degrees of Separation." Berg suggested that everyone is on average approximately six steps away, by way of introduction, from any other person on Earth. He argued that these six steps of separation should be at the heart of our 60-seconds in BNI; we simply should ask for our "dream referral," and by six degrees of separation we would always get the connection. While Phil was talking, I wrote my next 60-seconds to deliver to my BNI chapter the following week. Here is what I wrote, and delivered, two weeks prior to leaving on my bike tour:

'I went to the Phil Berg workshop. I learned about six degrees of separation. I would like to be introduced to Richard Branson. I know that if I met him I could inspire him to see the benefits of Treehouse Life—and to want to give these benefits to his children/grandchildren. He would want to add a Treehouse Life treehouse to his hotels. He would want to have one for his employees to be inspired. He would want to put a photo of one of our treehouses on the front of his Virgin branded in-flight magazines. He would engage with all our values of family and nature. He will like Treehouse Life so much that he would want to buy my company. We have two levels of separation in this room, from me to you and from you to all your contacts. For Treehouse Life to have the third degree of separation, I need to give you a benefit for you to want to recommend my company. If you connect me to degrees three, four and five (which connect me to Richard Branson), just think how much business I could give to your company if Richard Branson buys my business.'

When I returned from Vietnam and attended the weekly Surbiton chapter meeting, I had a referral introducing me to Sir Richard Branson along with his personal mobile phone number."

Think about how Paul now feels about the person who gave him this introduction! Do you think he now wants to help the person back? Do you think that after landing this massive opportunity that Paul is now totally motivated to help the person who gave him this introduction in as many ways as he can? Absolutely.

So let's look in more detail about the value of giving a connection. This is slightly different to giving a referral, as there are many different types of connections you could give to others.

Types of Connections

There are a number of different types of connections you could give to another person, some will be more valuable to them than others and it will vary from business to business.

1. A Referral Partner or Strategic Alliance

We have already covered these in Chapter 3 and Chapter 8. These are people who could lead you to multiple clients. Referral partner connections that you give, can be massively beneficial to others.

2. A Client or End Customer

This is an obvious type of connection, an end customer who goes on to buy from you, the difference you can make is the type of end customer and how valuable that customer is to the person who wants the connection. If you take Paul's story then one end customer for him was business-changing and very high profile. Many people will be happy with bread and butter end customers, the point is that any new customer is a valuable connection to most small businesses.

3. A Supplier

You may be paying over the top for a particular service, or you may have become unhappy with a current supplier, the same may be the case for the business contacts you know. By connecting people in your network with new suppliers and as a result help them to save money, get better service or save time the more you will be helping them and their business.

4. A Joint Venture Partner (JV)

Collaborate to accumulate! You may find that connecting someone with a business that they can build a joint venture relationship is a high valuable type of connection. Joint Ventures give the person and/or business exposure to a whole new target market and access to clients and prospects that without the 'JV' would not be possible. This is very common in the world of coaching, speaking and training. Collaboration partnerships can lead to massive opportunities for both parties.

5. A Mentor, Coach or Advisor

I would always advise someone to have a mentor or business coach, regardless of the size or state that your company is in. If you can connect people in your network with strong advisors, mentors and coaches then you indirectly are helping them, especially if the end result is a business changing outcome.

A couple of years ago, I had a web designer come to me looking for advice. He was running a work from home business and was working crazy hours and couldn't seem to get out of the typical small business owner trap, of wanting to grow but not being able to see a way to do it. He was debating whether or not to take on staff or to risk the additional overheads of a new office and a team to look after. I connected him to my mentor and business coach, Iain (who features in this book). As a result that web design company now employs 5 staff, has moved out of a home office and is smashing annual growth targets, the business owner is now delegating, working less hours and has a clear plan to move the business forward.

I know that this person is very grateful for the initial connection I gave him and today he is my web designer and my recruitment firm supplies him with new staff when he needs them. Givers gain in action again.

6. A Potential Employee

One of the ways you can connect people is by helping them to connect with potential staff members. Very often people will use their networks to find staff as this can be a lower cost way of hiring rather than the traditional recruitment agency. A person referred via a recommendation via trusted connection can often turn into a great employee. For other low cost recruitment strategies you can read this related blog: http://bit.ly/UtrXP2.

7. A Journalist

Giving someone a connection to a journalist that you know can also be a great way to give. Especially if the introduction results in exposure and PR for them. I often get referred to journalists when they are writing about online networking or face to face networking. I always thank the person who referred me to them as it always results in my businesses gaining massive exposure.

Networking with journalists on Twitter and LinkedIn is always a good idea, they are usually on the lookout for experts in various fields of expertise. In this type of connection giving activity, you compel both the journalist and the person you are connecting to the journalist to want to help you back in the future.

8. A Competitor

This type of connection, to a competitor, might on first glance seem unusual, however gaining an introduction to a competitor could result in some positive outcomes. For example, the sale of a business, a partnership or the ability to help each other, especially if the businesses are in the same industry but different niches.

I recently referred a Mediator based in London to another Mediator also based in London, although they did the same type of work, I knew from giving meetings with both, that they are great at what they do and can sometimes have too much work on. I also knew that they both specialised in different areas of mediation with a different target market. One was looking for clients in the legal profession and the other was targeting corporate multinational clients. I connected both and now they can pitch for larger accounts together and help each other out as associates when either is unable to take on a case. I know from subsequent follow up from both that this was a worthwhile connection.

Ways to Give a Connection

There are a number of different ways that you could use to connect people to each other, and with ever-changing technology this giving activity is becoming even easier. Here are 7 different ways for you to give a connection to someone in your network.

1. Through an Email Introduction

The best way to demonstrate this is to provide you with an example template to do so that makes both parties being introduce look good, which in turn makes you look good.

Example Email

Subject: Great Things Happen When Great People Meet!

Hi *[Insert Connection 1]* and *[Insert Connection 2],*

I am writing to connect you with each other, based on what I know about you both personally and professionally.

I am sure you could help each other in some way. Please see below contact details for each other as well as your respective LinkedIn profiles, I would suggest a Skype call or an in person meeting to start with.

Great things happen, when great people meet!:

[Insert Contact Details for Connection 1]

[Insert Contact Details for Connection 2]

Please let me know how you get on with each other as I am sure this is going to lead to some interesting opportunities for you both.

Kind regards

Sam Rathling

You can of course tailor this example email to each situation, but you get the idea. This is one of the most common ways to connect people and can give back great results from both parties.

2. By Social Media

You could use Twitter to connect two people together:

Example Tweet:

@jsmith meet @speakerbob, you should talk about collaboration as you both speak on similar topics and could work really well together

3. Through a Connection Request on LinkedIn

LinkedIn allows you to forward a profile to another person, so you could simply find the person's profile who you wish to introduce and connect with another person in your network, then forward their profile and send a message with it.

Note: You would need to be connected to both parties as 1st connections on LinkedIn to make this happen.

4. Through a Networking Event

If the connections you want to put together are both local, a simple way to connect them would be to invite them both as your guests to an upcoming networking event. This could be an event which you have organised or an event which you regularly attend. If the event is a seated affair then you could speak with the organiser and arrange for the two people you want to connect to sit next to each other. Alternatively use the open networking time at the event as a chance to connect them, arrange for business cards to be swapped and a follow up meeting to be set up.

A networking event gives you the chance to share with each connection why they should meet up:

Example: "Shane this is Colin, Colin runs a fantastic telecoms business and has helped me to save thousands in my phone bills over the last 12 months. Colin this is Shane, he runs a great IT company specialising in SME's although he doesn't currently offer Telecoms solutions to his clients. I thought you two could be great connections for each other so I wanted to introduce you both."

5. Via a 3-way Skype Call or Webinar

Technology is making it even easier for us to do business, using Skype and video webinars can allow 3 way conversations to take place, where you could invite the two people you want to give a connection to onto a webinar or Skype call to meet. You could either stay for the whole meeting or you could simply facilitate the start of the call with a similar introduction as you saw in the networking example and then leave them to get on with building a business relationship.

6. On the Golf Course

This won't apply to all of you, but a great way to introduce and connect people is to arrange a game of golf, where the primary focus of the game is fun and social. At some point the two people you are connecting are going to speak about business and are sure to find mutual ways to help each other by spending so much time together on the golf course.

7. In person, without you there but you arrange it

You could arrange for the two people you want to connect to meet up in a neutral location that suits them both, find out dates and times from each person and make the meeting happen. You could also suggest an agenda for the meeting based on the fact that you know both connections and what they could get out of the meeting if they explored certain areas.

8. In person, with you in attendance and you arrange it

Of all of the ways to give a connection to people, this is by far the most effective. If you arrange a meeting with two people that you know, like and trust, and then arrange for them to meet up with you also in attendance the results can be staggering. The reason this is such an effective way of giving a connection is that there is an instant level of trust between the two parties you are bringing together. Both of them know you and trust you.

They know that the person you are going to connect them with is likely to be a strong connection and also someone that can be relied upon. The relationship building takes less time because of the raised level of trust and the knowledge that you have brought them together for a reason. The fact that you are there means that there is a common ground already established. Finding common ground is usually one of the fastest ways to build a relationship.

An easy way to do this is to invite the two connections out for a lunch appointment or an early evening social drink after work. Put both at ease and again highlight the reason for bringing them together.

Both connections will really appreciate you putting them together and because you have given the connection you will find that both will be actively looking for ways to give back to you. Givers gain in action again.

Actions & Ideas on Giving Connections

1. Think of two people in your network that could work well together, but are yet to meet.

2. Choose one of the above methods to connect these two people within the next couple of weeks.

3. Find two people on your LinkedIn connections that you could connect using the forward profile function.

4. Send a "Great Things Happen, When Great People Meet" email to connect to people you know.

Chapter 14 - Giving Happiness

"Since you get more joy out of giving joy to others, you should put a good deal of thought into the happiness that you are able to give."
Eleanor Roosevelt

This is the Second Chapter in this book written Julia Foerster

This chapter concerns happiness in two areas of your business. The first is all about how to increase staff happiness, if you currently employ a team or are thinking about taking on staff. Secondly, we will focus on how you can increase how happy you feel in yourself, which can directly affect your business growth.

Staff Happiness

Employee Satisfaction finds its expression through interpersonal relationships, recognition and reward systems, and opportunities for creativity and self-expression at work, and it relates to intellectual stimulation and challenge, compensation and benefits, working hours, and the working environment.

Improving employee engagement has a direct impact on measurable business outcomes, because employees who are committed, engaged, attached to, and involved with a company are more productive, take less sick days and are more likely to stay.

"What's the best measurement for success? Happiness"
Richard Branson

This is one of my favourite quotes when it comes to thinking about the subject of happiness. The reality is that people perform better when they are happier, therefore, the level of contentment an individual feels toward his or her job is crucial for business success.

There are various different ways to increase staff happiness and employee loyalty and they range from helping employees see the bigger picture, to using training to increase confidence, to identifying what employees like, to establishing mentoring programs, promoting team building, building a supportive environment, encouraging open communication, retraining managers, and recognising employee contributions by providing a reward for above–average efforts. Other strategies include giving employees more control, encouraging social connections, praising employees' hard work, offering flexible working hours, making employees comfortable at work, and building strong relationships.

I had always dreamed of taking a trip around the world, although I was in a dilemma, because I was in a job I loved and could not see how I could fulfil my dream to travel and keep my job with Sam's business. Knowing how much Sam cares about our happiness as a team, I decided to talk to her about my ambition to travel. At that stage, I had been with the business for 4 years so I was hoping for a favourable response!

To my surprise Sam came up with the idea of me taking a sabbatical, the condition being that I could go as long as I put things in place in the business to cover the tasks that I was responsible for so that she didn't have to cover my job whilst I was away. After all she had spent considerable time getting to the point where she was working ON the business and not IN the business that she did not want to have to suddenly go back to the day to day operational tasks that I am responsible for.

So I spent the 6 months leading up to my trip, training other people in the team, improving our processes and getting ready to fulfil my dream of back-packing around the world.

I was able to take over 4 months out and come back to the same job, and was paid during my time away. It is now a company policy that all staff that have been with the business in excess of 4 years are able to take a sabbatical, just like I did. This is a very powerful way to engage your team, by helping them to fulfil their dreams.

You can see pictures of my trip and read some stories from my travelling adventure on this blog:

http://juliasroundtheworldtrip.blogspot.ie/

So we have established that staff happiness is important to your business growth, but before you can improve employee satisfaction, you need to know what to improve. The best way to identify opportunities to make employees happier is to measure employee engagement and employees' passion about their work and the work environment. You can do this through a simple tool, using a staff happiness survey which will help you to measure and understand your employees' attitude, opinions, motivation, and overall job satisfaction.

As such, it is important to run regular internal satisfaction surveys to gain on-going feedback and monitor the information over time.

To encourage open and honest employee feedback, you can use a third-party system that provides for employee anonymity, vital if you really want to know what your team think.

Staff Happiness Survey

A Staff Happiness Survey could include some or all of the following topics:

- Autonomy
- Benefits
- Communication
- Compensation
- Company Culture
- Creativity
- Employee Engagement
- Job Satisfaction
- Management Style
- Organisational Change
- Performance Reviews
- Recognition
- Safety
- Supervision
- Training
- Work Relationships
- Work-Life Balance

Below I am going to share with you some example questions to include in a staff happiness survey, you can design your own to fit with your team and your business or you can use free tools available to you, such as Surveymonkey where you can create surveys for free with up to 10 questions. Click here to learn more about Surveymonkey: http://surveymonkey.com

Some of the key questions you could ask in your Staff Happiness survey include the following:

Overall Happiness

How satisfied are you with your overall job? Scale from 1-10

Do you enjoy what you are doing? Yes or No

What areas of your work frustrate you? Text Answer

Do you find your work boring? Yes or No

How stressed are you at the moment? Scale from 1-10

Do you feel happy when you are at work? Yes or No

Do you feel proud to work for your organisation? Yes or No

Questions Related to Management

Do you think that the company you work for is well managed? Yes or No

Do you get along well with your manager? Yes or No

Would you say that organisation is a good organisation to work for? Yes or No

Do you feel motivated to do the best you can in your job?

Do you feel you have control over the important elements of your job? Yes or No

Questions Related to the Working Environment

Do you like the surroundings and physical conditions that you work in? Yes or No

At work, do you feel as if you can be yourself? Yes or No

At work, are you regularly able to do what you do best? Yes or No

Questions Related to Work/Life Balance

Are you happy with your current work/life balance? Yes or No

Do you feel that you have enough time, within normal working hours, to get your job done? Yes or No

Considering your efforts & achievements at work, do you feel that you get paid appropriately? Yes or No

Do you receive regular and constructive feedback on your performance? Yes or No

Questions Related To The Team

Do you like the people within your team?

In general would you say that your team is well managed?

In general would you say that teams within your organisation work well together?

Questions Related to Trust

Do you feel trusted by your manager? Yes or No

Do you feel safe to speak up and challenge the way things are done within your organisation? Yes or No

Can you influence decisions that are important for your work? Yes or No

Questions Related to Your Future

Do you feel that your job offers good prospects for progress in your career? Yes or No

Do you know what the next step could be for you, from the role you are currently in? Yes or No

Do you worry you might lose your job in the next six months?

Improvement Areas

In what ways could we as a business help to improve your happiness at work?

What ideas do you have for our next team social?

What would you like to change about your job or work, if you could wave a magic wand?

This is a selection of some great questions that will give you a really good insight into what your staff are thinking. You can then collate the responses and get an overall happiness factor.

There is one company you could talk to if you have more than 10 staff and prefer to get a more tailored approach to your staff happiness survey:

https://app.happinessatworksurvey.com

One of the most impressive corporate cultures I have come across, where there is a massive focus on employee satisfaction, is Zappos. CEO Tony Shieh, has written an amazing book called "Delivering Happiness", and in my role as Operations Manager of Sam's online recruitment business I have been able to implement a great deal of the learnings from Zappos into our business and culture. Zappos regularly survey their staff to gauge their happiness, because when their staff are happy, so are their customers. And this helps their business to grow.

According to the annual Society for Human Resource Management (SHRM) 2011 Employee Job Satisfaction and Engagement Survey which identifies the factors that are important in employee job satisfaction and employee engagement, the most important factors for overall staff happiness include Job Security, Opportunities to use Skills and Abilities, the organization's financial stability, the relationship with immediate supervisors, Compensation & Benefits, Internal Communication, the work itself, Autonomy and Independence, Recognition of Employee Performance, Safety, Corporate Culture, Flexibility for Work-Life Balance, and Relationship with Co-Workers.

Other factors include contribution of own work to the company's overall business goals, the meaningfulness of job, the variety of work, Job Specific Training, Networking, Organization's commitment to professional development, the commitment of the business to corporate social responsibility, Career Development and Career Advancement Opportunities.

A happy work environment has many benefits, such as increased morale and job satisfaction, a boost in performance and productivity, reduced absenteeism, sick days and healthcare costs, and better employer-employee relationships. More than this, having a healthy and happy workplace helps you attract potential recruits, and it helps you retain your best people.

A fantastic way to measure the happiness levels in any business is to include Staff Happiness as one of the goals in the weekly, monthly and annual business activity report. Let your employees know that their happiness is important to you and the business, and measure the overall staff happiness progress. I have seen this in action first hand and I know the impact it can have on the teams and the overall growth of the business.

Your Own Happiness

So now that you have designed a monthly staff happiness survey, addressing all the major areas of a happy and healthy work place, and you have reviewed the results of the survey and identified areas of improvement for your organization, this is the point where you have to ask yourself: How happy are you?

Your own happiness and mood as a business owner has a huge impact on your business growth. Running a company can be tough, stressful and time-consuming, and most people place all of their time, energy, and focus on all of the things they *feel they have to do*. Do you walk through your life feeling frustrated and stressed, finding too many things that just aren't working? When was the last time you deliberately made your happiness a priority for yourself?

Doing what actually makes you happy might feel a bit like a far-off dream but if you are an entrepreneur, the business should be structured to *enhance* your happiness. So how do you get there?

Get your Priorities in Order – Do what you love and always follow your passion. In business, focus on your business, your clients or customers, your employees and your systems first. Make sure everything is running smoothly and everybody is being treated well and feeling good. Then look at the money.

Focus on what you can control – Happiness is a state of mind! If you have made up your mind to be happy, you can always seek out the positive aspects of a situation and remain happy. Focus on what you believe in and change what you can change.

Build up financial reserves to help sustain the business in difficult times. Make money, earn money, then save money.

Create supportive and constructive relationships - Ensure that you seek out people who are happy and cheerful because being in the company of people who have a habit of criticizing is likely to divert your mind towards negative thoughts.

Make a Difference and Feel Better about your business and yourself – How is your business making a positive impact on the lives of others?

Show Gratitude – Make it a habit to say "thank you" and show your appreciation every single day, to people that support you, help you, mentor you, people that have hired you, referred business to you, asked for advice, transformed your life, and made an impact. Gratitude is one of the most powerful paths to happiness. You will have learnt more about this in 'Chapter 4 – Giving Gratitude'.

Rest and Recharge – Schedule regular time for yourself with family and friends and balance the various responsibilities and commitments that you have

Success and money can contribute to happiness, but happiness itself has a lot more to do with family, friends, love, and laughter than gross, capital, revenue, profit. As Richard Branson says, "money is a by-product of bigger, more meaningful goals such as passion, fun and wisdom. If you have fun, and do good, the money will come."

Be happy, because the success of your business depends on it.

So what measurements for success and happiness are important to you?

1. How would you rate your overall health?
2. Does your home environment stress or soothe you?

3. How would you rate your self-esteem?

4. Do you have at least a few supportive friends you can rely on?

5. Are you part of a church, support group, club, or other group that provides you with a sense of community?

6. Do you have any hobbies or activities that you get to do, on a regular basis, that are just for fun?

7. Are you happy with the role children play in your life?

8. Do you regularly help others and feel the positive difference you make in the world?

9. Are you satisfied with your relationship with your family?

10. Are you able to express your creativity on a regular basis?

11. Do you have personal goals for yourself, and live a life that reflects your values and spiritual beliefs?

12. Do you like what you do?

13. Do you feel you have enough love in your life?

14. Are you comfortable with your financial situation?

15. Do you know and like your neighbours?

16. Do you consistently learn new things, expand your skill set, and increase your knowledge base?

Take a moment to go through this list and really test out how happy you are right now. How much is this holding back the success of your business? How much is your happiness or unhappiness affecting your family life and/or your work life?

Happiness at work starts outside the office, so take the time to strive for balance because your happiness has more far-reaching effects on your life than just making you feel good. Your levels of happiness affect your ability to manage stress effectively, and they have a huge impact on how others interact with you. Focusing your thoughts and attention on what makes you truly happy, and making a point of looking for and acknowledging those things each day, will help you notice things working much better.

For example:

1. Better relationships: You come across friendlier and more relaxed, and as a result, you are more approachable. You will be better able to listen because you are less preoccupied and this is going to result in healthier, deeper, more successful relationships with your employees, your co-workers, friends & family.

2. Improved business performance. Your shift in focus carries benefits over to your overall work performance and more importantly, how you interact and manage your employees. You will find yourself thinking more clearly, more alert, making better decisions for yourself, the company and its employees.

3. Better health: An unhealthy body cannot be the home of a happy mind. It is important that you understand the strong link between physical health and mental happiness. If you are fit and healthy, you are likely to exude positive energy.

4. Improved Outcome. By law of attraction, you attract more of what you focus upon. Since you have repositioned your focus and attention on your happiness, you get more of the things that are working better and that make you happier and this will deliver more flow and positive momentum into your life going forward.

Ways to Create a Happy Environment

Here are some thoughts for you on how you might start creating a happy environment in your business:

- Hire the right people for your company culture

- Make it ok for people to have fun in their work

- Develop people through regular training, coaching, mentoring and provide opportunities for growth

- Care about the people in your business

- Support them and make sure they have what they need to get the job done

- Create a happier work environment wherever possible

- Have sponsored family days out

- Make both business and personal goal setting part of the performance review process

- Have regular performance reviews and give constructive feedback

- Say Well Done! Good Job! Congratulations! Sorry! as appropriate

- Make it OK to make a mistake once and then learn from it – fear of making mistakes is a major barrier to happiness at work

- Recognise your team – you will have read more ideas for this in 'Chapter 12 - Giving Recognition'

- Help employees connect with people that might be able to help them

- Celebrate employees' birthdays with the whole team

- Let employees pick their own projects

- Applaud employees' efforts with a standing ovation or applause

- Encourage employees to improve their fitness

- Share memories through a picture wall

- Have a quiet space in the office where employees can relax, take a nap or meditate

- Encourage employees to make their own decisions to inspire their passion on your behalf

- Include their partners when making contributions

- Give them the best parking space

- Let them have "Working from Home days"

- Encourage them to take some time off to follow their passions and dreams (like travelling)

The ideas covered in this chapter all add up to one thing, a happier you and a happier team which all leads to a better customer experience. Happy customers, means more testimonials, more repeat clients and more sales. All of this is directly linked to the growth of your business.

Some very small changes taken from ideas here can lift the mood of the people around you, your staff and your inner self. These small changes if implemented well, can make all the difference to the results you achieve once you really start to be aware of the impact of happiness on yourself and others.

Actions & Ideas on Giving Happiness

1. Design your own staff happiness survey and talk to your team about how their happiness is important to you.

2. Answer the questions in this section about your own happiness and make a decision for positive change. Are you working too many hours? Are you stressed out about money? Do you wish you could see your family more? What will make you happier in the short term and long term?

3. Who could you give happiness to? Take an idea from the list on ways to create a happier work environment and decide what you could do to give happiness to your staff.

4. Read "Delivering Happiness" by Tony Shieh, CEO of Zappos, an inspiring story about the growth of an amazing business which is packed with ideas to help deliver happiness to your team and your customers

Chapter 15 - Giving Education

"When I chased after money, I never had enough. When I got my life on purpose and focused on giving of myself and everything that arrived into my life, then I was prosperous." **Wayne Dyer**

This chapter is broken into three parts. The first part is all about you, and your continuous education as a business owner. The second part looks at how you can leverage your expertise and educate others to grow your business. Finally this chapter is about how you can give education to others and the communities across the world that really need it

Giving Education to You

I am a firm believer that every day is a school day, regardless of your age, type of business and current state of wealth, every one of us should be investing in our education through continuous learning and personal development. The late Stephen Covey has a brilliant quote that sums up why you should be focused on giving yourself an education:

"Your current knowledge base has a half-life of 2 years"
Stephen Covey

What this means is, every two years your knowledge base has halved, and 2 years after that it has halved again, and so on. If you learn nothing new now, the knowledge that you have today will be useless to you in years to come. A scary thought if you really think about this.

"Knowledge and skill are the only keys to the 21st Century. Knowledge has to be improved, challenged, and increased constantly, or it vanishes." **Peter F. Drucker**

Brian Tracy refers to this quote from Drucker, when he gives seminars about how to become a self-made millionaire. He can often be heard saying: "Today, you are just one skill away from doubling your income, greater profits and a better business."

I have followed Brian Tracy for a long time, ever since reading his book "Eat That Frog", and one of his top tips for success is to read books, articles or listen to audiobooks in your field of expertise for 30-60 minutes each and every day. When you read there should be no distractions, so turn off emails, phone and media to spend time to up skill yourself. He recommends reading the best-selling books about a skill you wish to master. If you simply copy what successful people do, learn from them and implement the tips you learn you can really give yourself the opportunity to learn new skills that can completely change your business and your income.

To give you an example, I have never published a book before, until this one. I always knew I had a book in me, and have always dreamed of writing a book on the topic of giving. I am sure that many of you reading this book, may be thinking that you too may one day like to write and publish a book. Now I could have hired someone to do a lot of the work for me, a Ghost Writer, Editor, someone to format the book so that it reads well on your device. Instead I decided that self-publishing was a skill I wanted to learn as I am a huge fan of reading. My husband is always amazed at the speed at which I read, and the volume of books that I consume. I love my Amazon Kindle Fire as I am able to tap into the huge array of books available on every subject imaginable.

When I started to write this book, I knew nothing about publishing on Kindle and other platforms. So I decided to learn. In the last 3 months, I have read 13 different books on the subject of publishing, marketing and formatting a book for Amazon Kindle. Every aspect of the publishing of this book I did myself, except for the cover design which I hired a freelance for, on Fiverr.com, so it cost $5.00 to secure a professional looking design which helped you to choose this book to read. I would not say I am an expert in self-publishing yet, and I do have a lot to learn, but I now feel that I have a solid foundation of knowledge on this topic now.

This is all thanks to some great books which I read on the subject. By choosing to self-publish 'GIVE', I have developed a new skill which I can use in all of my future publications as I plan to write at least 6 more books in the next 12 months. Now each book that I start selling can be more profitable, more quickly because my overheads and upfront costs are limited. I addition, I really enjoyed the experience and now hope to help others to follow the same path by sharing my new knowledge with people who I know that want to self-publish.

The information we have at our fingertips today and the access we have to great resources to get things done for us at a very low cost means that today's business owner can learn any new skill and get a great 'how to' article, video, blog or e-book at a very low cost. The barrier that always seems to get in our way is time. I know that it's not that you don't want to learn new skills it is that learning new skills takes time.

If you don't have the time for books and audiobooks, then you probably don't have the time to attend seminars and conferences either, of course they take time away from the everyday business of running a business! Plus these 2-3 day courses are usually expensive!

From my experience, you can't afford NOT to attend these amazing events. Yes, they cost money to attend, however the skill you need to master to take your business to the next level, could be in one of the sessions at the next conference or seminar opportunity. By immersing yourself in learning for 2-3 days you can really focus your efforts and get through an immense amount of learning in a short space of time, you never know, your next great business idea could come from a course just like this. That's even without considering who you will meet, every event is an opportunity to network, every opportunity to network leads to new relationships. These new relationships can turn into great connections that could take your business to the next level.

Giving yourself an education, investing in your personal and professional development as an Entrepreneur and Business Owner is vital. Take the time out to learn, whether it is through books, videos, seminars, audiobooks, articles, podcasts, it really doesn't matter how you learn as long as you are learning all the time.

Giving Education to Others

As a business owner in your chosen field, you probably have a huge amount of knowledge about your subject. Have you ever thought how this knowledge could benefit others and how you could leverage this knowledge to grow your own business?

Take a moment to write down all of the things that you are really good at in a professional capacity. Now think about where you learnt those skills and how you became good at them. It is likely that you learnt some of these skills through your education or reading books, some through practical application and learning on the job and the remainder are either self-taught or learnt from a leading expert in your field.

I guarantee you that there are people out there in your location, in your field who are just starting out in your industry, who would really appreciate learning from an expert. Could that expert be you? Would you have the confidence or ability to start educating others on how they could become as good as you in your field of expertise?

There are a number of different strategies you could use to educate others with your expertise, all of these have the ability for you to grow your business, due to the increased exposure that you receive as a result of giving lectures, presentations and seminars on your topic.

1. Create a YouTube channel with video tutorials and access a global audience

2. Speak at an event run by your industry or professional body to your peers

3. Get to know the local University or College lecturer who runs courses in your field and secure an opportunity to be a guest speaker for the course, do a good job and this could become a regular gig

4. Find out from your local Chamber of Commerce if members get an opportunity to speak to other members

5. Join local networking groups and share your expertise there, many are looking for guest speakers

6. Write a book and publish it on the Kindle store to share your knowledge (if I can do it, you can too!)

7. Create an account on http://slideshare.net and share your presentations with the world

8. Design a seminar or training event which you can sell tickets to for people in your industry

As you will see from this list, some of these ideas involve public speaking, which I know is not for everyone, so you may want to start out small first before moving on to a bigger stage, or just stick to the ideas in the list which do not involve getting up in front of a group of people!

You may not realise it now, but the information, knowledge and experience you already have is useful to other people. Now it's just a case of looking at how you could convert this knowledge into a useful platform for others, while growing the visibility and credibility of your business at the same time. If you can do this then you are sure to see your own profile grow and will attract more potential customers to your brand and will increase sales.

Giving Education by Giving Back

I have always wanted to give back in some way, this book is my opportunity to do so. In February 2011, I was fortunate enough to be invited to speak in Bangalore, at a BNI Members Day, a large conference with over 600 Indian Entrepreneurs. There are 80 million people living in Bangalore, a shock to the system when you come from a rural community with a population of just 1500, it really did take some adjusting to!

I was invited to spend a week with some of the most amazing business people, and got a chance to experience the wonders and delights of India. It was totally different to what I was expecting and I really found India to be a totally inspiring place.

I remember the smells and the sounds so vividly. I was amazed by the opportunities that exist in this incredible economy, and what I will treasure most importantly is the people. The relationships I built there with the most incredible people are to be treasured for a lifetime.

Whilst on my trip I was introduced to James Ambat, the Founder of a special project in the heart of the slums in Bangalore. James heads up the Building Blocks schools project, helping children from the most deprived and underprivileged families living in the slums to secure a future with an education in the English language. It is a project supported by the BNI Foundation (which you will have read about in the Chapter 6 – Giving Back).

The school provides food, uniforms and great teaching to children and gives them an education from the age of just 3 years old. On one of my last days in India, I took trip to visit James at the Bluebells School, the very first school to be built by Building Blocks, and now one of many being built all across India.

I was given a traditional Indian welcome, the children had made a beautiful necklace of bright, yellow flowers for me, and I lit a candle before entering the School.

I spent over an hour touring the school, I met the inspiring, amazing children and teachers and saw how just a few dollars can make such a significant difference, it can buy meals, materials and equipment that the school badly need.

The children were learning their colours, numbers, letters and places around, we talked about where I come from and they showed me where they live on the globe in their classroom.

They had even learnt a brand new dance for me and put on a show to some fast Bollywood music, they were clearly having an amazing time at the school, so happy to be learning and given the opportunity of an education.

After touring the school, 2 of the children took me to meet their Mother in their homes a short walk from the school. I will never forget the day that I visited the homes of the children.

The Bangalore sun was beating down on the dusty, uneven paths, and the raw stench of sewage filled the air. The children held my hand as we walked past animal faeces, rubbish bags and broken glass on the floor.

As we got closer to the river, where the worst sewage problems lie, there were hundreds of flies buzzing around our heads. I could feel the tears starting to well up inside of me, as I thought of my own children back at home and how lucky we are compared to the children here.

As I held back my emotions, I looked down at the two girls either side of me, swinging their arms as we held hands. They looked up at me smiling and so happy that someone had taken an interest in them.

They were very proud to introduce me to their Mother, as we approached their home.

I turned the corner to see what I could only describe as a shack, with cloth covering the front door, a rickety tin roof and clothes hanging up outside in the sun. The smell of sewage was very strong as we entered the dark, dingy space that the girls call home. I was later told that the worst of the sewage runs at the back of their house, and with no ventilation inside and no windows the smell really was overwhelming.

As I walked in to a space no bigger than my bathroom back at home in Ireland, I was introduced to the girls' Mother. She had a baby of just six months on one hip and a toddler no more than the age of 2 in the house with her holding her other hand. She has in total 5 children living in a space that you could barely stand up in, and would take less than 3 seconds to walk from the entrance to the back of the house.

Many of the Fathers have either left the slums and their family behind, or are alcoholics, who spend any money that they do earn away from the family home on cheap alcohol as their escape from their harsh reality, leaving the wives and children to fend for themselves in their cruel world.

It is thanks to projects like Building Blocks that the children have a future ahead of them, and who knows, maybe this start in life will help them to one day make a difference in the world.

By reading this book you have helped to give an education to these children. Following my visit to the school I made a promise to James and the children that I would find a way to help the schools project. On the flight home from India, the concept for this book was born and I began writing my first words of the first chapter of this book.

Today, thanks to you and many other business owners around the world, half of all of the profits of 'GIVE' go towards the BNI Foundation to help sponsor children in the school and to help build more schools like Bluebells across India in the poorest communities. I would personally like to thank you for making my dream of being able to give back in a significant way a true reality.

You can learn more about the Building Blocks Project here:

http://buildingblocksindia.org

You can learn more about the work of the BNI Foundation here:

http://bnifoundation.org

 The more people who gain exposure to this book, the more the children will benefit. If you truly did pick up some great ideas for your business by reading this book then word of mouth and sharing your experience of this book for others to be able to buy it, will not only be giving an education to your networks and people that you know in business, but will also be helping to give an education to children around the world who really need it, the entrepreneurs of tomorrow. Thank You.

Actions & Ideas on Giving Education

1. Choose an audiobook on iTunes or Audible.com on a topic related to business, buy, download and start listening to it in the car.

2. If you do not own an e-Reader such as an Amazon Kindle then download the Amazon App for PC, Mac, Android or Smartphone and start downloading books which are related to a topic or skill you would like to learn more about . Eg. Growing a Small Business, Leadership, Investing, Accounting, Social Media, Wordpress etc.

You can download the app for any type of device here: http://amzn.to/XTHawP

3. Look up the next seminars available in your industry, or look at the next business growth conference coming to your location from

a leading expert in personal and professional development and book your place.

4. Think about how you could use your knowledge and skills and give this to others by going through the list of 8 ways to share your expertise and decide now what action you will take from this section.

Chapter 16 - Givingpreneurs

"Giving people self-confidence is by far the most important thing that I can do. Because then they will act." **Jack Welch**

If you are reading this chapter then my hopeful assumption is that you have enjoyed the book, and I am delighted that you chose to read it and stayed with me through 16 great giving strategies. I know that you will make a success of your business if you are able to apply some or all of these giving strategies to your way of working.

I have been thinking since I came up with the concept of this book, how to describe the kind of entrepreneur that focuses on giving. I have chosen to use the word 'Givingpreneur'. My own definition of a Givingpreneur is:

"An Entrepreneur, whose main focus in their business, is on helping others through giving activities. The business owner and the people within their business have a giving mindset and know that all of their acts of giving will result in the growth of the business."

A few years ago I read Seth Godin's book 'Tribes' and now I have an opportunity to create a tribe of Givingpreneurs across the globe. If you would like to network with like-minded business owners, who like you are Givingpreneurs then you can join in a range of discussions on the following online groups:

The Facebook Group for Givingpreneurs: http://on.fb.me/13tjf8r
The LinkedIn Group for Givingpreneurs: http://linkd.in/WlK8Ux

Entrepreneurs around the world are coming together to help each other. If you want to become a part of the tribe of Givingpreneurs then we would love to see you participate in any of these groups.

Why not share your success stories, your ideas and experiences, or learn from others who have applied the strategies in this book and achieved success. You can network with like-minded individuals and who knows, once you start giving online, giving connections and giving support to each other you may just see additional benefits from being a part of the Givingpreneur tribe.

As the popularity of this e-book grows, I am keen to share stories of how this book has helped Givinpreneurs around the world. I would love to hear from you personally and if you would like to email me directly then please send an email to info@samrathling.com.

I will respond to every email although please be patient with the response. I only work 10 hours a week now, largely due to the success of this book, and my work/life balance choice which is to spend my precious time with my husband and 3 gorgeous children.

How Can You Help Me?

One last thing before you go. If you have genuinely learnt something new and/or plan to take action on the ideas you have generated from this information I would really appreciate a short but informative Amazon review.

This gift of a review on Amazon would mean more to me and the Foundation it gives back to, than you realise. By now you hopefully get that by giving this Amazon review, you will gain something in return. Maybe not directly but in some way you will benefit.

To your success!

I really appreciate your support, patience and time in reading this book and look forward to hearing of your success stories from the implementation of the ideas and concepts explored.

In the words of my BNI Executive Director and dear friend Sandra Hart, "because you have given of your time, so you shall gain".

About The Author
Sam Rathling

Sam is originally from the UK, and is now based in Cork, Ireland, she is married to Andoly, and together they have 3 children, Oscar, Maya and Liliana. Life is hectic, fun and spent mostly helping other people to achieve results through speaking, training and writing.

Sam is an Entrepreneur in the recruitment industry, with a focus on providing low cost recruitment solutions to give SME's a low cost alternative to the traditional recruitment agency via her business, Recruitment Magic.

Sam is considered an expert in online and offline networking, having contributed to best-selling book 'Building the Ultimate Network', she now speaks across the world sharing her networking success story, inspiring people to take action through giving and helping others.

Her expertise on LinkedIn, sees her travel the world delivering her popular LinkedIn Masterclass, a one-day practical course in how to achieve massive results with LinkedIn which is suitable for SME's and corporate sales teams.

In her role as a BNI Director in Ireland South & West, Sam helps members of her region to grow their business through the power of

'Giver's Gain'®. This is a role which she is passionate about especially due to the success she has had across 3 businesses since becoming a member in 2005.

Sam has successfully achieved what many business owners hope to do, which is to work less hours and spend more time with her family. She has successfully gone from a 70 hour week, to a 10 hour week, earning more money as a result.

Sam is currently writing more books which will all help you to grow your business through effective online and offline networking. If you wish to know when the next e-book is coming out and to hear all of the latest news from Sam, you can stay in touch by doing some or all of the following:

Follow Sam on Twitter: @samrathling

Connect on LinkedIn: http://ie.linkedin.com/in/samrathling

Subscribe to SamRathling.com: http://samrathling.com

19689462R00104

Made in the USA
Charleston, SC
07 June 2013